T0374213

Childhood History Repeats Itself

Letters to My Government

NOT FAMOUS

authorHOUSE®

AuthorHouse™
1663 Liberty Drive
Bloomington, IN 47403
www.authorhouse.com
Phone: 1 (800) 839-8640

Published by AuthorHouse 09/27/2018

ISBN: 978-1-5462-6190-2 (sc)
ISBN: 978-1-5462-6189-6 (e)

Library of Congress Control Number: 2018911475

Print information available on the last page.

Any people depicted in stock imagery provided by Getty Images are models, and such images are being used for illustrative purposes only. Certain stock imagery © Getty Images.

This book is printed on acid-free paper.

Because of the dynamic nature of the Internet, any web addresses or links contained in this book may have changed since publication and may no longer be valid. The views expressed in this work are solely those of the author and do not necessarily reflect the views of the publisher, and the publisher hereby disclaims any responsibility for them.

BOOK ONE

Childhood History
Repeats Itself

Table Of Contents

Preface

Finding the Subconscious

We carry forever within us our beginnings, our interpretations, misinterpretations, and our judgments. Our tomorrows are what our unconscious wants us to be.

The unconscious is the main part of the mind, from which is separated a little bit of the consciousness With so much to be unconscious, there is much sickness, which we are hiding from ourselves.

Very early painful childhood experiences, that are anti-survival, are shut away in the cellar of the subconscious. These memories become unknown to the conscious mind. This occurs because they are not understood and are too painful to deal with at the time, and mostly in order to deal with the rest of survival.

However they remain very active in our behavior although we do not understand why we do what we do. This way, the memory of the unsatisfactory experience is kept Moved away to not accept it and though hiding it away from ourselves The result is different degrees of irrational or not normal behavior.

Ask yourself. What memories am I hiding from myself that are fixed in misery? And which memories do I hide from others? What is it that makes me forever carry this burden of misery and feeling abandonment, stuck, fearful or other negative emotions?

It is that hidden unconscious part, hidden to yourself, that you need to find and free yourself from. At least not to die with it which is what most people apparently dread.

Ask yourself: Who am I? I am the one who talks to myself, all day, every day. What kind of a friend am I to myself?

You don't have to live a life that isn't yours. What others say you should be is based either on what they are, or the way they feel you would be of more value to them They are doing and saying what would make them happy

The identity trap is the attempt to make yourself be something you aren't. The intellectual trap is trying to deny your bad feelings such as hate, fear, jealousy, or guilt. Or holding back tears or good feelings such as infatuation, enjoyment or trying to make yourself feel good about something that does not make you feel good.

It is interesting to know what makes someone else happy but does not apply to you. If you are jealous about someone then that person is not right for you If you hate then it may mean you made yourself vulnerable to someone whose desires are in conflict with yours and he or she is using that power in ways that hurt you. If you are afraid it may be that you have put yourself in a dangerous situation that you can't handle.

This Book

During my lifetime I didn't have anyone that I felt I could confide in, and when I did, it was always misunderstood, so I talked to myself using the typewriter and later on the computer.

It was like I was living a conscious life and my unconscious life together at the same time overpowering my consciousness and damaging it, making it so hard for me to learn

I wrote all this material over a time span of maybe 80 years. This book is my thoughts of what I said to myself, my personal stories, memories and fragmented journals in search of finding my subconscious and understanding why I am who I am.

Maybe it is because of my age now, a secret I kept so long from myself, or maybe because much of present history keeps reminding me of my past. By facing the painful experiences I was able to partially let them go and accept who I am. This personal journey is about understanding, a path to acceptance and some freedom. I hope that by sharing this with you, it might inspire you to start your own journey into your subconscious

At this point since I lost most of my vision, I had someone help to put it together in some way to make it all more understandable.

Not Famous

Introduction

Yes, It Is Normal Not To Be Sane

I believe that it is normal not to be sane, because sanity is so rare. Insanity is so prevalent that it is recognized as normal. But, normal is not sane, for it is so infiltrated with insanities of various kinds and degrees that it is very difficult to even perceive the difference.

To be sane in an insane environment is very threatening So it becomes necessary to adjust within limits of sanity. In most cases a normal child is surrounded by various kinds and degrees of insanity, and has to adjust by adopting some of those insanities in order to exist with others, in order to feel safe enough to survive.

History is filled with proof of this. Even as adults, especially to survive in insane times in history, it has always been necessary to adapt to some of those particular insanities to be accepted.

When very young, insanities become ingrained into our unconscious, and remain with us as normal What follows is that some "normal" people are even more insane than some insane people are

Insanities

Insanities are a necessity in all human development. It can even be seen in animals.

Irrational and insane aspects are adopted for survival. This is inherent in our cultures and not recognized.

The inability to solve problems leads to irrational attempts with development of crazy areas for coping, especially when not understanding others, and not even ourselves.

The ability of using language and reasoning actually creates more complexities for developing insane areas

History is filled with many layers of examples. I have dealt with authorities such as lawyers, psychiatrists and political leaders whose variety of psychotic elements exceeds those whom they accuse of having them.

Infants are born into families and societies filled with irrationalities, with jealousies, with paranoia, with projection (finding others to blame for one's own behavior), and then have that to guide them and live with and then have no other choice but to learn to include this as a part of life.

Religions have been attempts to explain the unknowable and to help accept what is unexplainable in our social lives.

Preface

Paying My Debt

To this day, I don't understand why criminals pay their debt to society by going to jail. They certainly don't pay by having others pay taxes to support them. Who in society gets paid? It seems to me that society pays the debt that they owe. If society is owed a debt, then why make society pay twice? If the criminals are to make a real payment, what kind of payment should they make?

Well, this writing is my payment. I too owe a debt, a debt for being silent. I never stood up for my rights I don't want to be known Fear of being hurt is at least one of the reasons why some people write fiction, and even when it is not fiction, they can say it is.

This Book

I write negatively – satire and humor - subjective rather than objective, values and ethics rather than plot itself and about people and ideas rather than things.

Not Famous

Introduction

History Repeats Itself

We actually have no laws because they are reinterpreted by the social prejudices of the times If we have no fixed morality but have a fluctuating one that changes according to social and political and other prejudices then why pretend we have law? The U N. was supposed to be the hope of the world and is WHAT?

Capital punishment is seen as uncivilized because the state must murder the murderer. Cannibalism was accepted by society as cultural because it used to be that sometimes it was done out of need to avoid starvation.

Perhaps someday we will accept murderers as being guiltless if they will eat their victims again?

Youth started to worship the ignorant, the criminal, thus the age of the hunter has returned. The hunting instinct of man has returned in some of the young, since they are not allowed by the child labor laws to work, to struggle, thus they are returning to hunting. And since there are no wild animals in the cities to hunt and to make them feel powerful and needed, these young now choose to hunt human prey.

Since not all human prey live outdoors, the hunt has extended to inside the homes. All the laws of hunting apply here - such as the physically defenseless are sought. Will we have to use predatory animals to help hunt the human hunters, with hunting dogs to track them down in order to clear city forests, and city jungles in tall buildings?

While theoretically we don't have the right to be ignorant of the law - in the courts, anyway - we do have the right to be ignorant otherwise. This is what makes our political parties so expensive and wasteful. Because when it comes down to having the privilege and right to vote, our prejudices and wishful thinking is what does our voting for us, with almost any excuse as proof.

The right to be stupid, is what we get and what then follows is our right to blame others for our wrongs and non-thinking. This is what destroys what is good in our civilization, and we all suffer from this as a result, and without realizing why

Society and Evolution

Evolution and Social Grouping

Just as some animals are greater predators, the killing qualities of some animals are more prevalent in some human species. Animals have to abandon their offspring when a newborn is expected, and be on their own.

Early men were prey as well as predators. The hell they went through in their evolution, for survival. Human predators destroyed their ancestors by killing them for food

Hunting with weapons predated man. Our precursors hunted so we evolved as man. We must have used primitive weapons.

Speech began with hunting and a human kind of social organization Hunting involves weapons, which require manufacturing of weapons. Use of tools requires teaching and teaching requires language and capacity for organization.

When males hunt and females gather, the results are given to the children and rest of the family. When the birth of our conscience occurred, our memories led to tradition, and tradition led to religion.

The weapon fathered man. He raised the animals - all are evolutionary products of the success of the hunting adaptation. Agriculture has dominated human existence for less than one percent of man's history Man became man because of his years as a hunting animal. Therefore it created the desire, even the need and certainly the emotion to destroy life as it came in the original package. Killing is part of man

Man - with his upright position, his opposing thumb, and his pushed in face The result is that man has the adrenalin of a hunter and the digestive system of a herbivore. We have to cook our meat to break down the proteins.

When we are young every living thing becomes an educative toy Even a Siamese kitten, scores of generations removed from necessity, cannot resist killing a mouse, even though it will not eat it. The same happened with our young man-ape play trying to copy adult activity

Boys have interest in hunting, fishing, fighting and games of war, which they developed in play. At some point, grown men started killing for fun, from necessity to recreation.

Sports can be seen as a ritualistic physical prowess.
Religion can be seen as a reutilization of fear.
Warfare with predators is society endorsed.
Hunting is now sports. We were born with eyes,

heart and brains of slayers, and as killers we live.

Is it any wonder that man loves to kill?

Cannibalism Exists

It may be that evil is related to cannibalism, still as part of our early history. Cannibalism still exists in various ways, not only in humans actually eating each other, as originally for survival.

History has grown on lies. Just as disease feeds on germs, Cannibalism is the original method of life for survival. The big fish eat the little fish, some animals eat other animals and humans eat animals Those that eat other animals or those then eat plants And worms nourish on plants etc.

There are other forms of symbols of cannibalism that involve tearing into those whom one is jealous of and though removed directly, are symbolically evident.

A more extreme example of cannibalism is the German cannibal Armin Meiwes, who was arrested involving a victim, who had responded to his advertisement, wanting to be such a victim. He received more than 200 responses of others who willingly offered themselves as victims

The past history of mankind is closer to some of us genetically more than to others. This can explain so much of genocide, history, and what is not understood

3

Pecking Order

The natural pecking order of whole groups, one race against another is automatically a pecking order, and therefore gives the individual a natural pecking order

If those children come in contact with a different cultural background and are taken out of their own normal pecking order.

Natural rank and dominance among individuals can be completely interfered with by the imposition of laws over the individual dominant rank by the government. The higher and lower degrees of dominance by laws, the arm of the government occur in schools and in the family.

Laws are artificial and unnatural restraints of dominance among people. Since the government is and has to be in the first rank of dominance, so weaker ranking people can borrow the dominance of government thru the laws and oppose or overwhelm the dominant – and thus it is as if the house comes falling down

A couple of white hunters can go through Africa with some guns and successfully oppose the dominant (primitive).

Dominance comes into play constantly and is opposed by many things Money buys power and allows people to overcome natural dominance of others. Ideas, culture, religions, ideologies, dogmas can frequently vitiate the normal and natural pecking order in complex societies.

In primitive societies there is no interference with the normal pecking order causing frustration allows people to overcome natural dominance of others. Ideas, culture, religions, ideologies, dogmas can frequently vitiate the normal and natural pecking order in complex societies

In primitive societies there is no interference with the normal pecking order causing frustration and unhappiness when people are kept out of their pecking rights being deprived of it. Laws, dogmas, customs, ideologies, prevailing trends may interfere with someone enjoying their pecking order.

Europeans have recognized and decreed these tendencies here which they consider infantile and retrogressive and use these methods to weaken the dominance of the government, knowing that the entire structure of civilization is based upon the levelling of government. You either accept the government or defy it – by creating subcultures.

Subcultures deny the government and take powers for themselves. They demand total power for their group and use the group to wield the power of that group as a weapon against the government.

Question Of The Century

What is the question of the century?
It is not about the economy
Not about the progressive political party.
It is not the conservative party.

It is not about the wasteful expenses that are not covered
It is not about what we would imagine it is
It is the question of how are you
Just observe the different answers of the question
How are you?
It is behind the question that the answer lies what is causing
the lack of knowing how are you.

Communication

To communicate requires more than language, more than really listening. It requires how the other person thinks, and being able to follow and accept the irrationalities and peculiarities, and possible history, and not negate but to accept. It is so easy to sometimes say something that even surprises the one who says it. It is easy for a very truthful person to say something that is incorrect and suffer the consequences of an incorrectly spoken remark or to make a misunderstood statement that though correct and well intentioned, is interpreted very wrongly.

The New Meaning Of Words

I still have difficulty understanding the new meaning of words. Like: "How are you?" Is now not a question but means a form of hello. For me it is still a question, but I have finally learned to accept it by answering: "Yes, thank you." And the questioner seems to accept it as if I answered, which I didn't.

Retarded children are now called exceptional in schools. It seems to be tied up with the high payments given to "teachers" of these children who are not only not exceptional, but their teachers are even less exceptional.

Well similarly with our dining room workers, it is with the word rare, which is misunderstood by them, and I keep wondering what is the new word that I do not know? When I asked for liver, I asked could I have it very rare? She said of course you can, and that is what you will get I didn't know the new word so what I got was a scorched dried out inedible liver. When she placed it on the table in front of me, she proudly said: "This is what you wanted, it is very rare." When I left I asked the one who acts as the head, what the correct word for very rare was. She laughed and said she will find out I decided while she is not finding out, and never will, I must wait until I learn the correct word before ordering it again.

Where do these new meanings come from?

The same applies to politicians who are regressive but they call themselves now progressives. Can it be that the new politicians create them? Do the old words mean the opposite of what the new words mean? If this is the answer, then I must ask for it scorched when I mean rare That is an easy answer if that is correct

Poor doesn't mean what is not even known today. Poor often means less than some, sometimes more than many non-poor, and sometimes just not rich as the richest.

Intelligent often means knowing how to makeup very big lies while smiling charmingly.

Copying Advertisement And The Truth Lost

Copying advertisements, truth gets moved further and further away until it gets lost

Language helps to do this by changing the meanings of words Words that meant what we know they were changed to be the opposite. Like retarded is now called exceptional and regressive is called progressive We make bad meaning good when they are not.

This keeps on until we have only confusion. And to most people good becomes bad and bad becomes good Some people use their religion to help with the lies. We then regress to the times before scientific proof of facts when we simply believed only what we liked to believe and what we wanted as being the real truth for everyone. And when this occurs within the government, it then teaches the people to do the same

Suppose all advertising were abolished?
Would there be more honesty about products?

The World Has Become An Advertisement

The world has become an advertisement. It is in, and by, newspapers, television, in our mail, in just everything. It is so prevalent that I can't always recognize information that is not meant to be an advertisement.

Since advertising does not have to be the absolute truth, but is expected to have embellishments, exaggerations, etc. in order to show up what you want to get across. The same methods of expression become part of our language and thinking

I wondered how all the ads can sound so alike to me as if one person made them all up for everyone and for everything. It seems to me, that instead of their being what used to be, a one God for all religions, there has now developed instead a one God of, and for advertising.

Real People

When I call on the telephone, I first have to ask: "Are you a real person?" to know if I am talking to a recording of "one message fits all"

I am truly surprised when I find out I am actually hearing a real person. I am so impressed that I just spill over with friendliness, as if I just found my true soul mate

If that doesn't happen - or before I discover it to be a real person - I never know what I might say - and I do say all sorts of things that I would not say if I knew. To know what I said would surprise me more than anyone else

I do not know how different I become when I am talking to a non-person When, and if, the real person gets my message, I have no idea if anything was understood. I do not even know if it was heard or listened to.

Since the real person is used to not being real, he, she, or it doesn't feel the need to be real to answer anyway. After experiencing the joy of being a recording, and not having to be there – at least not there to listen - and if heard, or even listened to - he, she, or it, is not there for answering. Being so used to not being real-'it' now no longer feels the need to be real anymore.

Obesity Past and Future Evolution

Obese human beings have been discriminated against, and sometimes still are. But I believe this may be an evolutionary stage, with the result that skinny people will become discriminated against in the near future, especially the ones that remain small. Some are already feeling they are, or can be stepped upon since people are becoming so tall and big. The big people are much too strong for the customary frail sizes to compete with.

I became frighteningly aware of this when I was squashed against a very sturdy heavy gal sitting next to me in an auto when her arm merely brushed against me, and it felt painful, as if a very heavy iron bar was weighing me down, and I felt afraid. I thought if we would have an accident, that before getting killed by the accident, I would be crushed to death by her falling against me.

We seem to be returning to past history in many other ways, and at the same time we may be going back to the time of Buddha, when part of his superiority was his obesity, which at that time was considered divine.

Since the majority of people are developing great strength in their height and width, and majority attitudes and ideas become the norm, this may happen very soon.

I have no idea how, but it will change our understanding of biology and medicine, certainly change our understanding of what is good for us, what is healthy, that is now considered not healthy. It will influence new beliefs in medicine when doctors will tell us what we should do to abolish old concepts of aging.

Bones especially are stronger in these people of the future, and even now. Already developed - evolved so that many of today's problems regarding such fears will be wondered at, and believed to have been alleviated by new imaginary medical concepts.

People Believe In The Idea Of Equality

People believe in the idea of equality. But, equality of what? Do you know? Are people born the same? Why not? Do you want everyone to be the exact same as you? Do you like everything about yourself?

Do you want everyone to be better or worse than you are? Or the way you were born, or the way you have become?

There is a common, philosophically childish belief that if everyone in a society had the same amount of money that it would then make people equal. Many people really believe that rage, hatred, and all crimes are caused by poverty and that by eliminating poverty we will cure all evil people and evil behavior. They ignore the reality that many people of wealth commit crimes, and that many very poor never do.

People who believe that money is the cure of all evil in society also believe that having equal amounts of money is what makes people equal. They ignore the fact that no person can possibly be equal to another, that all people have differences, both by birth and by experience. It would also displease them immensely if everyone were exactly the same as themselves

Most people seek someone or something to blame, instead of seeking rational solutions for dissatisfactions, in order not to feel like the helpless infant that was completely dependent on others good intentions for survival. This infantile error for adulthood is always seeking a scapegoat, and is a serious part of inequality.

It is inequality of justice, of fairness, to each other, beginning very early within the family, and remaining fixed in our unconscious, which then continues outward onto all others from then on. It is the inequality of justice and rationality that makes people unequal in the most meaningful way.

This inequality does not get corrected by money. In fact, many people with lots of money use their money to create more injustices. Throughout history, they have often been the ones who have waved the banner of poverty to create the most and greatest injustices, and this continues to go on and be so

People continue to believe that poverty is the cause of all evil, and therefore, money is the cure of all evil. The terrible things that some people do to others is often excused and blamed on poverty This is a historically continuous lie. It is not that poverty does not exist The poor I have known never advertised it, as many not so poor do The truly poor do not look as if they were bursting with excessive energy, as the now called poor do.

People who believe that money is the cure of all evil also believe that having equal amounts of money is what makes people equal They ignore the fact that no person can possibly be equal in all ways to another All people have differences, by birth and experiences, as well as, circumstances and knowledge.

Not only is the causal excuse of poverty used, but also the twisted use of fairness, as a fault created by society and its responsibility to correct, by equalization of wealth alone, calling that fairness. Poverty often brings cooperation

Jealousy, privatized or socialized, is the Achilles heel. If everyone were poor, we as a human race could never do so much evil We would have to use our energies to forage for food and children would be happy to be of use, instead of just playing and having open mouths to be fed like birds without hand if the poverty is the fault of the rich, would poor people be rich if there were no rich people?

The Flag Of Poverty

Poor people like these don't usually ask, let alone demand, anything. They try to better themselves by their own efforts, instead of using their energy to reproduce future criminals and those who enjoy forever using the flag of poverty.

Justice vs. Law how each criminal act could be compensated for, by the most just correction of it

The education of the distortion of history. A terrorist, a dictator, a thief, a destroyer of all that is good is honored as if he were a hero at his death and the world sends its representatives to honor him with dishonest praises. Praising evil by all who mistake it for diplomacy.

DNA existed before civilization. We live in the future and feel guilty about the past. Must be in the present to change the future and the past. Root of any sickness = blocked light in area, life force of god, we have to contact the energy. The desire to change is the important need We are all inter-connected. We are never alone. Jealousy is the worst

Evil eye means taking the energy from the other person. Need to create a shield where negativity can't get through to protect yourself. Words have consciousness; a solution that is complicated can't be true. Energy cannot disappear

Poverty often brings co-operation, unless there is jealousy. Jealousy, privatized or socialized is the Achilles heel. If we were all poor, we as a human race, could never do so much evil We would have to use our energies to forage for food. And children would be glad to be helpful instead of just playing and having open mouths to be fed like birds without hands

Most human beings seek a scapegoat, someone or something to blame - instead of seeking solutions for dissatisfactions, and not to feel helpless and completely dependent on others for survival This irrational infantile error in adulthood is always seeking a scapegoat. This is the most serious part of what creates inequality.

It is the inequality of real justice, of real fairness, to each other - beginning very early within the family, which continues outward onto others from then on. It is this inequality of what is fair and just that makes people unequal in the most meaningful way.

Money does not correct this. In fact many people with a great amount of money use their money to create more injustices. Throughout history, they often have been the ones who have waved the banner of poverty to create the most and greatest injustices.

The Nouveau Riche And The Nouveau Poor

We used to speak only of the "Nouveau Riche", never expecting that the poor could change very much as to be classified as old or new types. Poor people were classified as just always poor as if it were an unchangeable inherited reality Today, however, we have not only the nouveau riche, but also the "Nouveau Poore".

The old poor never looked as well fed and strong as the new poor do today. The classic poor used much of their energy to forage for food; the new poor use much of their energy to forage for sex and fun, like some of the old riche and most of the "Noveau Riche" do.

Today the "Noveau Poore" can't imagine what it is to be like the old poor. In those days their children did not wait around to be entertained while being cared for. And just like the poor used to work for the rich, today many people, including the government, now work for the "Noveau Poore".

The "Nouveau Riche" used to be looked down upon by the old rich when there were not so many of them. Today even the classic, inherited rich have accepted and combined with the new rich in similar behavior and friendship, especially when it comes to entertainment and finances.

A great many of the "Nouveau Riche" are entertainers. The newest, therefore the "Noveau Noveau Noveau Riche" are those who entertain by playing games of ball.

Some other noveaus are outside of the social scene so far because they entertain and are entertained more privately, with the new technology.

We hear of terrible and evil things going on - all explained away by the word "poverty". It's not that there is no such thing as poverty, but the most really poor I have known never advertised their poverty as they do today

If more people were poor today – like during the great depression - there would be less crime and theft and envy as we have today. It is increased by the advertised belief that poverty by itself is the cause of all problems – when poverty actually brings more cooperation and kindness and sympathy, instead of jealousy.

The "Noveau Poore" have now become a model for reference, and glorified almost into a new kind of religion Poverty has become the new scapegoat to blame for everything, and has even been made by some into a new kind of messiah that has to be hanged and crucified in order to then be worshipped and blessed - before the new creation of the world of Love.

How To Get Paid Well For Being Stupid

I have always been told that "Ignorance is no excuse before the law," but I have been finding out that this does not apply to everyone. This is the way it was proven to me that stupidity is not against the law for everyone

For example, this sweet woman who loves to get a nice big full cup of hot coffee for her breakfast as she quickly rushes off to work in her auto mobile. What better place to put it than on her lap between her legs so that her quick moving car can splash it around a bit and prove that it is full by spilling over into her lap. (I do wonder if she teaches her children to do it like that?)

Not a stupid enough thing to do, she finds a lawyer who loves stupid people. The kind of lawyer who loves to pick a stupid jury, especially those who hate people and companies richer than themselves, although they love the product the company sells. The result is that the jury awards the woman millions of dollars for being stupid. Rewarded so very well for her stupidity, don't you think?

Now I am wondering if such a jury who knows how to blame others for their own stupidity still loves this woman whom they made rich? Or do they now hate her too for being richer than themselves?

Not All Dummies Are The Same

The Dummy books are a great idea and have become big business because there are so many of us, especially when you combine the genuine dummies with the intelligent dummies.

Some of these books are not so easy to understand because some are written for the intelligent dummies, at least in part, or maybe even written by the intelligent dummies. This is too bad because then you have to be one to understand one.

There are many differences between the genuine dummies and the intelligent ones For instance, genuine dummies know what they know and know what they don't know. They don't have to fool themselves or anyone else.

Intelligent dummies are not like that at all. They think they know everything and they always think that what they know is correct, especially when it is not

Intelligent dummies are in the forefront everywhere. In the stores, answering the telephones, in businesses, in schools, in the professions, and esp. in government agencies. They are the dispensers of information and the ones who answer your questions. They make up answers to questions in order to be polite and make you feel at home. They sound as if they really believe their own answers, which they have just made up

They can even pretend they don't hate you when you question their answers. They are experts in knowing how to pretend they know it all. In a way, they decide what your questions ought to be because very often they really answer their own questions rather than yours. And finally you realize they can't understand your question at all, and you must accept that as the final answer

The best thing to do is to answer your questions yourself. Some genuine dummies do that well naturally having escaped the hazards resulting from education and training. This is how the saying "a child shall lead you" was born. The wonders of it are that some genuine dummies remain that way instead of outgrowing it and becoming an intelligent dummy.

Children's Minds

We have been raising a generation of grown people with children's minds and memories without rational judgment. They remain children in their minds.

The helpless infant that was completely dependent on others for their good intentions for survival. This irrational infantile era for adulthood is always seeking a scapegoat. This is the most serious part of what creates inequality.

Not To Be Mistaken For Grown-Ups

There is such a fear of being mistaken for grown-ups, that they even conceal from themselves the fact that very small children are also grown-up in many ways. In my day it used to be that older people really believed that small children had no feelings and no mind at all. In fact, I used to have to pretend that they were right, not to embarrass them, and so I acted as sexless and as mindless as I was expected to Now that it is known and expected that they do feel and think, the children themselves try harder than ever to hide this as soon as they start showing signs of growing up

At this time, in spite of all this, there are some very small ones who refuse to go along with being either good or even being children, and they play the opposite kinds of games. They do everything possible to prove what mature thieves and killers they can be, and they show the old people even how to have sex. I'm not sure if they do this merely to have fun and play, or also to help teach them.

Advance Or Regression

In trying to understand some of the present changes, I wonder if its meaning is evolutionary advancement or just an adjustment to what has happened and what is.

It used to be that people wrote poems to expose a thought or feeling. Today it becomes a song and is expressed by the jumping up and down. Is the jumping due to crowding, or some evolutionary reason I don't know yet Is it done in a form of aggressive expression? Is this aggression or exercise people want the government to replace their parents? Is this an advance or regression of physical growth or emotional?

Change

Young people want change expecting change always to be better. Change occurs whether you like it or not. The most difficult thing is to change oneself. When we are very young is when we are formed and it is very difficult to change later on in life.

Society and Psychology

Einstein

I wonder what Einstein thought when people who were less intelligent said to him that he is intelligent?

Maybe just like the dinosaur that became too complex and died off, maybe that is what is happening to the human being.

Now The Insane Are The Sane

People do not know who is sane and who is insane. So some years ago they decided to let everyone out of the asylums.

Now the insane people have all the answers. They say let us decide and rule. So now the insane are the sane and are able to accuse and blame the others for everything that is wrong

Normal People, Geniuses and Idiots

Some normal people are crazier than crazy people are.

Some examples: Two small boys playing with their sheet of white paper, which they then folded and called guns, for which the normal school authorities punished them by expelling them.

When another small boy in grade school pulled an attractive little girl's curls, he was accused of sexual harassment. Before schools became this normal, that was considered a form of teasing and admiration for the little girl.

Normal people often consider geniuses crazy and crazy people are often considered normal by normal people. When normal people think that crazy people are crazy, they like to punish them for it

There are also brilliant idiots. This very intelligent and highly educated N.Y lawyer, who is also heard over the radio, is a truly brilliant defender of irrationality. To a great many people, irrationality is normal.

Successful Relationships

Successful relationships depend more on how curious the partners are than on how smart they happen to be. Also if both are non-curious, then I Q. also does not matter

Like-mindedness attracts and opposites repel in long term, but in short- term, relationships can be physically attracted.

Incompatibility

I must be asking myself wrong questions - since it can't be answered simply enough. About who is evil It may be that when 2 incompatible people live together they both have to be evil to each other I am evil when I allow myself to be abused, used, made unhappy and for staying around and putting someone into the position of wanting to behave evilly toward me Perhaps we must act evil to each other in order to live together. Perhaps just the fact that there are such divergent personalities that exist with different needs and different ways of thinking, perhaps that is what creates evil behavior. For in some cases there is no other way of coping with extremely different types of people, different species, coping with each other, often even in the same family, even between parent and child.

Jealousy

Jealousy is the greatest motivational aspect of human beings, next to survival, and often even supersedes it. When this happens, it even works against survival. It is much more destructive than other inherently damaging attributes of human nature

Jealousy motivates everyone in endless ways - and is a driving force in life - both constructive and destructive Since it is more often destructive, it is important to be able to recognize its danger.

In my experience, when others may delight in knowing that others feel jealous of them, with me, I felt it was necessary, (and I was willing), - to eradicate bits of myself- to help others not feel this way about me in order for me not to be afraid of them

Sex As Part Of The Digestive System

Some people really think that sex is part of the digestive system. Most male persons really believe that for a female person to like him at all, she must show it by instant sexual feedings.

They act as if science were wrong and the heart does not lie in the heart area, and that the mind does not lie in the mind area, but that the heart and the mind lie in the sexual area, and of course, that the sexual area is part of the digestive system.

Smoking And Public Sex

Smoking is like public sex. You can't smoke without making others smoke your smoke, just as you cannot get excluded in the presence of public sex. Both smoking and sex invades all that is present.

Looking For A Matchmaking Heart

I met a lady through a mutual friend, and I was invited to her home. It was a beautiful day, a beautiful beginning. I was impressed with the others' elegance and her ability to express herself. What a nice new friend!

After a long, very friendly, and very satisfying give-and-take, both interested in similar activities and work, by some accident our conversation touched upon political matters, exposing our different viewpoints.

The new friend was displeased to learn that I was not politically liberal like her. She explained her preference to me by stating that liberals have a HEART, and she demonstrated this by placing her hand over her own heart

She continued on to stress her ability of having a HEART for people, and didn't want to hear anything further from anyone not having this same kind of heart If you are not politically liberal, you cannot have HEART; you cannot feel for anyone.

With the same hand with which she had touched her heart, she waved the no-longer-to-be-friend away. Like a mosquito being chased away, I was no longer a human being to her, and she had no HEART for me any longer.

It was now apparent to me that I will never get to know what that kind heart was like, and the no-longer-friend who believed herself as absolutely right would never learn about me, not having her kind of matching heart

It is very sad that friendships – and even civilizations – can be destroyed by human emotions imbedded in childhood that are not remembered but remain influencing our lives forever.

What We Think Affects The Body

Since what we think and feel affects our body, the mother's body is sensitive to receiving impressions Infants can tell how people react to them, if they are wanted or rejected A baby nursed on negativity receives the most poisen Parents do unto their children as was done to them, which they didn't want done.

What the world is today hostility is raging. How negative and more powerful, 100 persons may enter the room and complement you and your first reaction may be amazement and self-consciousness, then a guilty pleasure. You feel guilty for fooling them, because they don't know enough and because you know they don't really mean it But let one person be negative and you believe it.

Doctors, Godlike Role Play

It is fear, not guilt, which is troubling, thus, we are deprived of feeling healthy guilt, by not taking responsibility for rectifying responsible hurts to others. To the child, and therefore to the unconscious, the physician pronounces death to what is bad

It's All Relative

There are different kinds of minorities, aren't there? Kings are minorities Murderers are minorities, or at least they used to be. Saints are minorities. Are some minorities good and some bad? Or is it all relative? This relative thing is very interesting. You can always change it by saying: "Oh, well its all relative" In that way we can change the meaning of anything.

Do Roaches Have a Right To Live?

"Do roaches have the right to life?" I asked myself It was a time when we were inundated with a particularly strong and very healthy, new variety of roaches in our city of N.Y.

Roaches are intelligent, have a very long history that goes very far back before humans, are fully and beautifully formed, and functioning. Right now, so many of them have chosen to live comfortably with me in my apartment, and eat at all my food.

When they look me in the eye and run toward me rather than away from me, I feel guilty to kill them So I talk to them and tell them "I do believe in your rights, but the problem is that you are taking away my right to privacy, as well as presenting me with risks because I do not know where you have been and with whom before me. I tell them; "I'm willing to feed you if you allow me un-invaded space."

But I do not think they are concerned about my feelings because, if they were, they would not alarm me so with their exuberant multitudes If they weren't so arrogant, they could even avoid showing themselves to me, since they have endless hiding places

I do find it very difficult to see them as loveable and huggable. And while I may also not be loveable to them, they make me feel that I am very huggable to them because they like to crawl onto my arm when I don't aggressively and hastily reject them

Dogs forgive; humans don't.

Dogs will risk their lives for their owner.

Freud said a person can be in love with someone without knowing it because of blocked access to his emotions, and the cause of human misery lay in the trauma of our childhood

Dogs feel more intensely than humans Humans have ambivalence and can experience deception Dogs are without ambivalence.

Society and Religion

The Idea Of God

God is used in trying to understand what is not understood, what is not known

It is used in so many ways by different types of people as attempts to understand ones self, others, and all that is not known by different ways in the attempt to understand the unknowable, and to seek a principle of unity with others

The idea of God is to perceive an idea of the world. It can be misused and expresses man's capacity for evil.

The mystery of God to the mystery of man himself

Do Christians Need Jews To Save Them?

I had heard a preacher on television say that the world will be saved when the Jews believe in Christ as their God - that is if Jews become Christians

Why is it that these Christians need Jews to save them? And no others? Why do Jews have to save Christians when

Jesus has already saved them once? Why does this have to be repeated? And why must Jews take on the sins of Christians to save the Christians? What would then be expected if all Jews became Christians and still didn't get saved? What would then be demanded of the surviving Jews? If no Jews survived would that help the Christians?

I heard Russian communists say that in order for communism to work in Russia, the whole world has to become communists

And, if all Jews did become Christian to save the world, would the world become communists or would the communists become Christians due to the Jews having become Christians and having saved the world?

What Is A Jew?

A Jew is a person who is chosen. Chosen to be the scapegoat of the world throughout history. As a result, the Jew has been without a country, with a history of roaming from one country to another. Depending on when the political or religious rulers need them and welcome them up to the times when they reject them, feeling they need them no longer.

Similarly, more recently, it occurred to a Jewish doctor, whom Castro had considered very valuable until be decided that this doctor "knew too much", and he decided to have him killed. (Cuban doctors in the Mercy Hospital told me this, but he was forewarned by someone, and was able to escape.)

Similar to why the Romans had Jesus crucified. It was the same with all the made up accusations against Jews throughout history. After a ruler would pretend to offer Jews freedom in order to get what he needed and wanted, he would then enslave them and begin their destruction. It is a continuation of a form of cannibalism when eating the brains of the victim was the chosen reward.

If Jews served no other purpose in world history, they would still serve the purpose of being the scapegoat for the entire world - a very convenient substitute for realizing their true dissatisfaction and hatred of themselves, of their parents, their rulers, or their Gods

At these times, they do not consider Jews human when they are alive, but then at times consider them Gods when they are dead. When the country is in trouble they hallucinate that it is the Jews that are the cause of all their own unhappiness, even of all their own evil thoughts and deeds.

A New York Times article states: 'In Poland, a Jewish Revival Thrives - minus Jews! Every June, a festival of Jewish culture is held to pay homage to the people who once lived there and contributed so much to Polish culture. They sing Jewish songs and dance Jewish dances."

So you hate the Jews when they are alive, but how you love them when they are dead! Throughout history when a country has been in trouble, you invite them, and when they come and start to trust you, and because they do their best, you are envious and you murder and destroy them You pretend they have horns, that they take red blood – while you are taking theirs – and make white flat bread magically out of your red blood!

You have taken one of them, and not only made him your God, but then even made him non-Jewish, divorcing him from his religion, and claiming him as the beginning of yours. You do everything to make Jews fear you when you mention his name You do this to always remind them of what you did to him and to so many of them, and are ready and able to continue to do so again.

After murdering him, then you made sure to make them the victims, by teaching your lies everywhere, and continuing to tell your children, and those children to their children Teaching that he was not one of them, and that it was not you that had him murdered and that Jews must feel forever guilty for your deed by turning their other cheek to you so you can be ready to strike them again whenever it seems necessary or convenient so that your frustrations have someone else to blame for all human mistakes and unhappiness.

It is very easy for some of you to forgive yourselves - all you have to do is say a few Hail Mary's! In a religion that expresses symbolically that wine is the blood and a wafer is the body of God, this is still the expression of past-inherited cannibalism that goes very far back as part of past survival

Because of this social cannibalism keeps getting continued by the use of Anti-Semitism. Yes, Anti-Semitism is the result of inherited social cannibalism which recurs and recurs very strongly when problems of survival becomes problematical or questionable, and which occurs periodically whenever it gets caused by wrong political and economic choices, even when imaginative threats of survival occurs. Of course social cannibalism only begins with Anti Semitism, it does not end there, even though awareness is forever lacking.

I am "The Jew"

Blame the Jew! Blame the Jew! The Jew is at fault for everything that bothers you! I am that terrible Jew!

Are Jews a religion, a nationality, a race or none of these? Or is a Jew a Jew because a non - Jew considers him that? And is able to blame him for all his bad feelings? Perhaps many Jews would not have remained as Jews since they were without a country to defend them, often without a religion of acceptance, and certainly without being a single race!

Even people such as Vanessa Redgrave, and Gore Vidal, although they do not know me, hate me because I am a Jew. If I am a Jew - what am I? Or am I what Vanessa Redgrave and Gore Vidal, say I am- only that I am a Jew

How many people know me? What I am is what they say I am, though they do not know me. Do they even know what they themselves are? Do they think I am what they don't want themselves to be? Though they do not even know of my existence, they do know they are against me.

Someone once told me that he could always recognize a Jew by looking at his eyes. Is this a look of distrust, of fear, of pain? And what causes it? I also wondered why he told me that he could get a lot of money for his little daughter who was with him, because she is a Christian child in great demand He was an American moneychanger in South America, of German descent

The historic Edith Stein was born Jewish and converted to Catholicism, and as a devoted Catholic, was taken from the church to be murdered for having been Jewish, though she was a Catholic. What is your explanation?

I Am The One You Hate

I am the one you hate for I am a Jew

In my memories are such as my first day in school. I was a 6 years old child and it was my first day in school. A boy in my class, his name was Lawrence, I can still remember his name after so may years, at the end of that first day, as I was leaving the school, he yelled: "Jew Bastard" as he kept throwing stones at me, the way the religious Arabs do now in the Mideast.

Every morning we pledged allegiance to the flag, to God, to the country, which I did, but to the vocal children, it wasn't my country or my God, even though I was born here and some of the others were not I felt like 'the man without a country'.

Several years later we moved to upstate New York, as I walked miles along the country road to grade school, and later to high school, I passed neighboring houses with signs "No dogs or Jews allowed". My brother has one of these wooden signs that he acquired somehow. This area of New York many people today call the Jewish Catskills. Actually it never was, except for two months in the summer when New York City people invaded the low priced summer resort types of getaways.

We lived there all year and few other Jewish farmers like ourselves The Jews were summer people, and they supported the area, when it wasn't good enough for others. Until much later when it achieved popularity that it was a bargain and before poor people became rich enough to travel

The New York City people never learned country behavior and never learned about the wooden signs.

I remember well a lovely little girl who lived near the school we both attended - we became best friends. At Easter she asked me to go to church with her during the Easter celebration. My mother told me to respect all religions, and I would hurt her feelings by not going. We sat together happily. Until, at some point, the priest said that the Jews killed Christ. My special friend never spoke to me again. When we passed each other at school, she hung her head, and would not look at me.

Jews Have Been Hated

Judaism expects and demands a greater maturity than many people are ready to accept. It is much easier to reject this degree of maturity by hating the Jews for it.

Jews believe that all people should take responsibility for themselves, and in self-blame Jews have been hated for this. Today even very many Jews hate the Jews because of this. They became accustomed to wanting things to be easier by turning to Christianity because it doesn't expect self-responsibility and self-blame

There is a famous old saying that "The greater the lie, the more it is believed, the greater the truth, the less it is believed

Not only did Hitler know and used this, so does our attractive president know and use it Freud made a study of how irrational thinking works and why

Resented Because Of Their Talents

Lack of physical affection, a love of inflicting pain (Arabs) In England, at the time of Shakespeare, love of your kids was considered inappropriate. "Spare the rod and spoil the child" The children tortured chickens, burned cats alive, and pitted animals against each other. All this was fun. Later humans developed love of sports. Arabs allowed men to hold hands but not with women - like most of us. The Moslems see only their good sides and not their dark impulses, see them as belonging in their enemies.

When someone does something bad - if he is a Jew - the news always mentions that it is a Jew, but never or calls or mention that it is a Christian who has done something bad When a Jew does something great, they never mention that it is a Jew. Never do they say Einstein the Jew, or Freud, the Jew. When people resent Jews because of some talent, perhaps forced to develop for survival when jealous, they should be told to get themselves persecuted and perhaps then they will do as well.

The hardest thing about being a human is to understand what the others are and what they really mean rather than what they appear to mean, acting a certain way and not knowing what is inside- their hurts, their misunderstandings. While you misunderstand them, they are also misunderstanding you, and then one misunderstanding builds upon another That applies to me and the pain is all that's left with me, and that grows and grows. If you don't get it right from birth, it keeps going wrong Those who deliberately give pain to others are more "Normal" and better off.

Reverend Jessie Jackson is so holy that he doesn't need to use a toilet. He defecates from his mouth. Farrakhan's holiness, leader of the religious group Nation of Islam, however, consists of a superhuman iron intestinal tract that converts his food into bullets and daggers, which he ejects from his mouth.

Why Christians Hate Jews

Education was one of the principal reasons why the early Christians hated Jews. Eighteen centuries ahead of the rest of the world, the Jews had compulsive public education. Early religious commitment to literacy was the secret of continuing Jewish success and the source of consistent envy. The Jews could carry their religious traditions with them into exile.

For the next two thousand years, the Jews were the only literate nomads on the face of the earth.

Literacy also allowed the Jews to develop a unifying sense of their own history The ability to read existed almost a century before Jesus was even born. Every Jewish village was required to have a teacher to train young men to read religious scripture.

An example, using the same wooden bowls for milk and meat products is a bad idea in the hot desert climate Therefore it was the first written public health code in the world, which appears in the Hebrew Bible, the Torah.

The Ambassador Christian College states in one of their pamphlets: "In the 14th century the bubonic plague struck Asia and Europe because of its poor sanitation. The Jewish physician Balavignus instituted a clean up movement among the Jews and the rats left the ghettos. As a result the Jews mortality rate was less than its non-Jewish neighbors But instead of emulating the hygienic measures, its people accused the Jews of causing the plague and poisoning the wells and a general massacre was launched against the Jews! Balavignus was persecuted and tortured to make him "confess" that he was responsible for the disease!

Descendant Of Job And Abel

I am a descendant of Job and of Abel and often find myself surrounded and affected by the descendants of Cain. His descendants are more abundant. The world is mostly affected by the Cain's. Some of them are mixed and are very deceiving (they are psychopaths) to those from Abel The descendants of Cain with their genetics and the spreading of mixtures of all the Cain's

Jews And Hitler

Referred to the bible as the monument history of mankind. To cleanse his own soul Hitler saw himself as continuing the work of Jesus, the work against the Jews, as a Messiah.

People deny that Hitler was religious. Himmler was even more religious, also Roman Catholic, which is religious practice of fundamentalism. Hitler's mother had a strong faith and remained Roman Catholic.

1945 May 6th mass held for him honoring Hitler, and the church helped Nazis to escape to Argentina. The church had cooperated with him and also helped and encouraged anti-Semitism including Catholics who had Jewish ancestors.

The Jew Jesus

Jesus has been persecuted over and over again in the form of other people

Whenever a scapegoat is needed, a Jew can be picked out to be the new Jesus - over and over again, the repetition of History

Some Americans have been demanding a new crucifixion – that the Jews be the victims for all immorality. These Americans have been setting themselves up as the judges of morality to appease the more immoral demands of the judges who judge not themselves

As Rome of Yesterday, these Americans were and are demanding that the Jew be the victim of all immorality, cheekily demanding the Jew to turn his cheek, bullying the Jew into his roll of masochism, martyrdom.

He feared only because he was anti Semitic. He was obsessed with it, as his original sin that Jews were Satan-born.

In John, the Jews are the children of Satan. The snake symbolism of Satan struggle of power of church over state and words from New Testament attributed to Jesus by St. Paul

Evolution of Emotions

The evolution of emotions is not easily recognized when it turns into destruction of physical evolving. The mind is able to find ways to deny reality and is able to not even connect the result with the cause Mostly this is a psychological way to avoid blaming oneself, not to see ones own faults and to avoid feeling guilt and finding excuses as if there were reasons for someone else's fault, thus putting the guilt on an innocent person or group away from oneself.

Some of the early followers of Jesus, a Jew, were able to thus use the symbol of Jesus as if he were not one, in order to want to destroy all the others to make themselves feel superior.

Christ, the Greek word for Messiah, became a symbol for their right to persecute the other Jews This need to make oneself feel superior is always connected with jealousy. Many Jews also forgot the connection, and after endless persecutions began to symbolically identify the word Jesus with the cause of their deaths. However, today many Jews are able to realize that, in spite of the fact that the word Jesus for generations and generations meant swords and daggers against them, that by this time, civilization has gained and, to some extent, risen above it.

Just as there are different degrees and changes evolving in different animals, so it is in human evolving. Some children become more and more like the parents in accepting their negative traits, while some offspring learn from that and take on their positive traits, and fewer who are able to reject the negative destructive ones.

When people began calling themselves Christians, and had adopted parts of Judaism and mixed it with Pantheism, they began to persecute the Jews. Then many Jews even tended to forget that Jesus was one of them because symbolically he became the cause of their being persecuted He was not only murdered by the Romans, but the Romans, who then dared not to take the blame for what they did and called him God, then distorted history to turn the blame on the ancestors and descendants of Jesus. Always most humans who are guilty or jealous find reasons to put the blame of their hurts and inadequacies on someone else.

Just as a child who is neglected and mistreated by a parent turns its hatred against another sibling, and just about anything available, because the parent responsible is more necessary for its survival.

Praying For Love Or Justice?

People pray for all sorts of things. If I would, or could successfully pray, I would pray for fairness, for justice. I would rather have fairness than love. Perhaps the word love is sometimes used as a substitute word for fairness?

I don't trust "love" All sorts of things are called love. Desire is often called love Sex is usually confused with love Love often turns into hatred, and revenge

I don't think there can be love without fairness, without justice. By justice, I do not mean to confuse it with equality. To me, religion - at least my religion - is a matter of justice, nothing else. It is something I do not experience very often in relationships with others. It seems to me that all my life I keep looking and waiting for, and falsely expecting it - as if it were my human right.

It is because of this desire, and expectation of justice, that I am chronically pained If I did not expect it, feel it as a need, I would be free of most frustrations and hurts. I sometimes think I must be at fault for thinking this way

Today is Easter Sunday. Christianity believes that Jesus died for other's sins. In the same manner of thinking, I sometimes feel that I am at fault for other's wrong doing. That if I always knew the right thing to say, and do, then the people I know would not be at fault in their behavior, and would not suffer or cause suffering to others. While I am aware of my unimportance, I apparently feel that I am important in this way as to be at fault for not being able to help others be more righteous and just.

Most people don't like it, don't want it, and resent it - without realizing what they resent in me. Even when a religion stresses this, it is also resented by those religions that do not.

In general I have been often resented more for my virtues, rather than for my faults. It would not be so bad if it weren't that I seem to mingle with such persons, by choice or habit or attraction? Of course all this starts very early in life and doesn't get turned off easily

Some people call it Karma. But the Yogi I once knew - when he was interested in me - told me I was an old soul - almost pure and ready to be complete, and therefore my last incarnation. However, when he became disappointed by my lack of physical response to him - he then changed his thinking and said that I had to have had a terrible Karma to be experiencing my present life That is what I find "love" is about.

At least I have had numerous destructive experiences relating to what is called "love." And many times merely because I, as the recipient, am either unaware of the other person's feelings or unable to return it in kind to all those in need, or desire, of it. In many cases, when love has not been returned the way the person wanted it, then extreme hatred follows with a vengeance

In the name of love so many abuses occur. I wonder how many different kinds of things are classified as love?

Long ago I saw a foreign movie about a young girl living in a small agricultural town. She was the prettiest, kindest, and wisest – and therefore greatly admired and loved by all In the end, people came forward and attacked her with their pitchforks. She was loved and admired for all her virtues and hated enough to have to die for having these virtues. Such is within human nature - and is one form of love.

But back to the belief that Jesus died for people's sins - yes, he died because of people's sins, - not for them. To think that he died in order to remove the sins of others is not only a perversion of rationality, but also the greatest example of true injustice

If this is not seen for what it is, how can children be taught about justice when they are taught to believe something so irrational? And how can adults expect justice when they had been taught how to avoid it - by putting their blame where it does not belong?

Society and Education

The Right And Wrong In Education And Law

When I attended Columbia University and took some courses at Teachers College, some professors who were teaching future teachers, insisted that I cannot-must not-judge anything as being right or wrong. Right and Wrong is only relative, they insisted, and is not to be judged.

The teaching of right and wrong as erroneous started that long ago and has been influencing our present-day thinking and behavior.

The law defines insanity as not knowing the difference between right and wrong. Thus if insanity means not recognizing the difference - and at the same time, ideas should not be judged as right or wrong because ideas of morality are merely relative-then it follows that insanity is normal.

If it is therefore normal not to know the difference because it is only relative - and at the same time the law judges insanity as not knowing the difference - then the result is the mental chaos which we have in our schools, in our streets, and in our homes

Education colleges concentrate on methods rather than content of truth, values, justice and fairness.

How To Improve Our Education System

Even trying to improve our education system we must first start with justice and law.

I have taught in public schools It is not the amount of salary that makes an education system good or bad. Money is the least important factor in making or breaking education

First, education for what? If laws, lawyers and judges and courts are not concerned with truth and fairness, that country cannot have truth in education. Nor can it have respect from other countries. Our laws are not concerned with justice What is justice?

With the present corruption and the so-called political correctness of lies which is extremely noticeable in politics, in advertising, and its influence in everything. One of the overlooked influences on greeting with "How are you" and you are supposed to lie and say "great" or "good".

The "I love you" is another example. I love you to death is more obvious about what might be meant by love. Or "Sweetheart, my darling", perhaps it is said before it really becomes true. Maybe this is a middle evolutionary step before it really becoming true.

What Is Justice?

What is justice? Love others is preached everywhere. Why is it that people have to be told constantly to love? Can a person love who does not know or understand justice?

Some religions have befogged and blurred the concept of justice The newspapers are full of concern for improvements, of elimination of juvenile delinquency and improvement of education.

ALL PROBLEMS ARE PRODUCT OF LACK OF TRUTH AND JUSTICE.

The choices are only between justice and power Where justice is not the first consideration, it must be power and might and ignorance.

A society is only as good as it is just - not riches. Factual and technical knowledge is very important but not enough Military strength is important but it is certainly not enough. Education is very important but it is not enough for educated people can do evil more excellently.

The right education, which has to include truth and justice, is the beginning after knowledge of what justice is.

Society, Politics and Economy

Social Worker's Paradise And Our Insanities

Our insanities have also changed. Today we have the social workers paradise of insanities.

All the problems, if man will be cured by social workers, who will descend upon us from the moment we are born to guide us

Human beings cannot be allowed to develop in the world by themselves They must be coddled from the day they are born by non- human super social workers and receive the advantages of the money the social workers will get for doing this.

Parents are not to be trusted, and should be guided by social workers even if they too had parents The entire surroundings must be refashioned and reshaped and no expense spared because the money used will create superior knowledge and capabilities.

All school dropouts can become social workers. And everyone has the right to become president because that is the definition of Democracy

American Children

American children are brought up in a Democracy, which is known as the best of all, and have learned to associate it with the word democratic party. They are unable to recognize evil. Some are even very bored with everything being so much the same and want 'change'. And to them change means of course even better. So every one of them thinks more democracy is better than what they now have

However there are masses of people who hate, have been brought up from two years old to hate what American children were brought up to love. The children brought up to hate are very intelligent in knowing ways of expressing their hatred. For instance the muslins, as well as all non-democratic groups of people, understands that if they call themselves democrats, which will win votes. This is so easy to do because so many people confuse Democracy with the words democratic party

Mass psychology does the thinking and irrationality wins. The present Muslins learned that all they had to do was call themselves democrats and the White House is theirs. Then they went further and said they want to work with the opposing people and they just sit by and wait for them to agree and continue its new democratic ruling by continuing to want to work out the disagreements with the others. This "offer" consists of nothing but waiting for the others to agree, to get tired of waiting and coming to agree with them.

Projection And How To Win

I was familiar with bullies such as destructive parents, children in gangs, criminal mobsters, and dictators who disallow and confiscate weapons of self-defense, etc.

Of course lawyers who destroy justice for innocent people whom they damage by destructive verbal bullying in order to win.

Only recently have I witnessed how our present government won over all rationality by the use of verbal bullying. This method included the motto of the bigger the lie the more it will be believed. Even Hitler acknowledged that he made use of this fact about human nature.

Freud called it projection. Whatever you don't like about yourself, you see those traits in others who are not that way.

What happened in Russia when the ruled became the rulers of the previously ruled, as well as the previous rulers? It is like making the children into the parents.

What We Don't Like

It is common to not believe what you don't like.
So politicians use this and create more problems to civilization

In order to recognize people that lie and deceive, you need to have learned to lie yourself

If you do not lie you do not recognize if someone is not telling the truth.

Whose Fault Is It?

Now, for instance if I have a sore foot and ride on a bus and someone steps on my sore foot, and it makes it worse —is this the fault of the bus company for being crowded, all the people inside the bus, or outside of it, or the person who stepped on my foot, or the fact that I had to use the bus? Or what caused him to step on my foot - the bus lurching, the driver, the bad roads and the way the bus was constructed? Or was it the man's attitude, his way of behaving, or the fault of the sore foot? Or was it God's fault, or society, or the local government? When a child throws a bottle out of the window and someone outside gets hit by it - who is at fault? Is the bottle company at fault, the parents for making the child, for having windows, and to have open windows?

The Right To Blame Others

While theoretically we don't have the right to be ignorant of the law - in the courts, anyway, we do have the right to be ignorant and stupid otherwise. This is what makes our political parties so expensive and wasteful.

Because when it comes down to having the privilege and right to vote, it is our prejudices and wishful thinking that does the voting for us. Finding some part that could be useful for oneself and using almost any such excuse as proof. That is what our money gets used for!

The right to be stupid is what we get What follows then is our right to blame others for our mistakes in judgment. This is what destroys what is good in our civilization We all suffer from the result, mostly without knowing why.

Money Never Solves All Problems

American people still want to believe that money can solve all problems.

The lesson by Russia has not convinced enough people that money is not the real solution for problems. The American idea of creating the new "Great Society" by using (thereby misusing) money created more problems

Now, when all the new "health benefits" will be enacted, we will learn that using money to solve everything does not work. In fact, it can, and has, caused many more problems. What is wrong with our present health-care system was actually created by using money as if that would solve everything - as a substitute for solving human problems. By substituting lack of money as the cause for all problems, the need to understand human problems is abolished and forgotten.

Then using money is the easiest to misuse and is causing endless more problems

We wouldn't have so much crime by children if they had to learn how to survive hardships instead of learning how many luxuries some have - mostly useless

How To Balance The Budget
And Avoid More Prisons

Our government has been working so hard to find ways to increase productivity and employment. Our President Clinton has even been traveling abroad in search for such a needed solution to stimulate our stagnant economy. He has been unsuccessful so far except for diet pills, fertility pills, and anti-abortion pills

Our private sector has also failed to provide us with such a needed product due to its selfish concern about high taxes and regulations.

I think that only a product, which is universally needed, could automatically solve all our economic, as well as social, problems today.

Everything can still be remedied if our President (preferably before election) would only recommend that our government instantly patent and manufacture a made in-U.S.A, mechanical parent as a replacement for our present method of breeding children without parents (This method had been copied by us from the farmers' way of breeding chickens from eggs in heated brooders without the presence of the mother hen.)

Our factories would soon be working overtime on making computerized loving parents with all the proper parental skills and all "Made in the U S A" labels.

It would even make our Unions very happy and minimum wages would simply explode by themselves.

Our production of criminals would then be so reduced that the need for more prisons would be unnecessary, and the **forever-increasing budget would get a well-deserved rest.** Most of our government officials could then go happily on vacations

The only resulting problem I can see is the jeopardizing of our **Right of Freedom to do crime and spread falsehoods** and that might create a serious problem for lawyers.

Tipping Is A Contagious Disease

Tipping is a form of payment that is an offshoot of slavery. In my early days, and still engraved in my thinking - accepting, or even being offered a tip was something to be embarrassed about. It felt like an insult. To me it was akin to begging, bondage, or prostitution.

While sometimes it can even be well deserved for a service, not otherwise compensated for, basically it is something that is not meant to be a true payment - and it usually is not - but is a kind of reward for either being pleased - or more often, pretending to be pleased. In this way, it is not something earned but a reward for being satisfied - or even worse as a bribe - and which is much more common.

Some people are appreciated more for giving large tips, while others who do not, may be even more appreciated. Some people are not appreciated no matter what they do. In that way it is also an offshoot of gambling.

As bribes, it becomes inflationary, because bribes are never enough Like a fever, the more you do, the higher the fever. Sometimes the bribe is given out of fear, to avoid being harmed in some way, similar to paying off a bully, or dictator. Sometimes it is a form of advance payment for future favors.

In addition to all that, it is like a contagious disease in that everyone has to catch it and pretty much outdo others in order to feel correct and worthy, or not be embarrassed and feel guilty.

Bush, The Real Serpent

In the past the serpent had to go all the way to the Garden of Eden to do its damage. Today the serpent just keeps on smiling as he runs to the internet and TV to do the same.

But instead of a tree, he keeps saying: "No, it's a Bush." He keeps repeating Bush, Bush, Bush. Bush! And they all cry back: "Yes, Bush, Bush."

Bush becomes the real serpent.

Abortion Laws and Politics

It is interesting how little our politicians show concern about protecting people's lives from predators and yet fight so much to protect fetuses. Can it be because we have so many laws protecting the criminals and murderers, that it is necessary to preserve possible fetuses in order to provide the predators with new populations for continuing their rights?

I don't like normal people - that is, normal in our society, I feel there is something wrong with them.

Anti-abortion-People, who eat eggs are committing murder by not allowing the egg to hatch into a chicken.

Obama, Our President Is A Successful Orator

Our president is a successful orator. He is very active and attractive. In his speeches he keeps saying the opposite of what he means, and he is believed because he keeps telling us what he knows we like to believe. He is successful and admired for it.

Our president is excellent in knowing how to keep blaming others because in that way he keeps others from blaming him.

There is the famous old saying "The greater the lie, the more it is believed, the greater the truth, the less it is believed". Not only did Hitler know and use this, so does our attractive president know and use it Freud made an important study of how irrational thinking works and why.

Mirror, Mirror On The Wall: Who Is The Fittest Of Us All?

Proof for the theory of natural selection for the survival of the fittest is the criminal. This fittest of all is not only well specialized in such abilities, but also familiar in all areas of survival so as to be able to constantly adapt to new changes to fit any new type of crime made available by evolutionary changes.

Have you ever known of a time or place where criminals went out of style or ceased to exist? I have not. The criminal seems to be born knowing how to survive off others, and therefore is always able to adapt to all changes by finding new avenues to fit new types of crime

In my neighborhood the examples of this evolutionary phase is very noticeable and worth learning from. To not be one of them is certainly dangerous and limiting to the survival of the unfit like myself.

In fact, most of the people I meet are shifting little by little in that direction to escape becoming a victim. To avoid non-survival, they have also begun to practice victimizing others, starting first with friends and relatives

I have a friend J., and to prove her good intentions and friendship, she showers me with feelings of guilt as to my unfitness. The result is that I, an unfit, am becoming more and more in the outcast class, for lacking such fitness for survival.

The way it looks to me right now, is that I am nearing my extinction: proof that criminals are truly the fittest of us all because they are extinction proof.

An Outlawed Subspecies

Did you know that in Florida there exists an outlawed subspecies of human beings? I'm one of these undesirables. I've become a misfit, a subhuman, a throw back to the ape when it first became human and started walking upright. I am therefore a threat to our mayor and to civilization because I do not drive an automobile, nor like him, do I have a chauffeured limousine.

My mayor is so focused on moving traffic that all the old-fashioned safety rules of lights were eliminated to have four-wheels crisscross quickly and to eliminate useless people who still need to, or try to, walk.

This is being done to eliminate all undesirables on two legs to make room for more four-wheels and thus not to remind people that they got off all fours to walk upright on their hind legs, and now have come back on all fours, but attached to wheels

We pedestrians (who use only two legs) are bad reminders of the early attempts to stand up. In Aventura we are more than expendable, and we need Dr. Kevorkian to help clean up this disturbing vestige- or else we must choose {which we deserve) to be mowed down by this rushing, rushing, crisscrossing traffic.

To beautify Aventura for drivers, the mayor cloned Barbie-doll-like trees along the boulevard and placed an expensive metal stand to block right of-way passages for willful, desperate pre humans like me.

I also had no idea how much Miami is a parking lot and when I got information about how to go somewhere, I was told that the address is behind a parking lot (but not told about how many parking lots were in front of and behind the ones in front of before the one that was in front of the one I was to find the right parking address

Future Species

For the skin and fur for clothing The pain and torture of an animal crying, knowing it will be murdered by the smell of death, remains strongly etched in my physiology, in my memory, in my entire self. Maybe people will develop plants and trees that do not require human nutrition - to be related to predatory solutions for food.

Some species will develop the use of scrap metals and pollutants and other waste products and thus clean up the environment for a new group of species, and thus changing from being a predator of live beings to purifying the previous evolution. And the Jews who fit in the category of the chosen will be eliminated by the survival of the meanest

The evil ones consider themselves blameless. Since they deny their own badness, they must perceive others as bad They project their own evil onto the world they see it in others.

A Solution For Our President

How our President can change the problem of diversity in Democracy (financial, political, religious and social differences), which he told us he wants to do

Since Adam and Eve lost their heavenly childhood in the Garden of Eden by eating the fruit of the matured tree of knowledge, which resulted in their becoming aware of sex and that they have to labor to get their food, we, their descendants have become compulsive about both food and about sex. The greatest of evolutionary change from plant life resulted in the problems of today.

Animals depend both on animal and plant life for survival, while plant life depends only on the sun, the rain and the soil for survival. This evolutionary change in food is the root of all present evil If that need would be eliminated, all our problems would disappear again

If only Adam and Eve would not have made that terrible mistake of eating that particular fruit of knowledge, or perhaps better still, not eaten at all? This eating progressed to our eating meat, which started with the need to kill in order to get the meat, and then developed many new ways to kill. Once we learned how to kill, then wars became easy and necessary

If we didn't want such food, there would be no poverty and no need for politics and politicians, and certainly no little Red Riding Hoods with bad wolves to frighten little children about being eaten

If people would simply return to living again like plants, using the sun and rain, and with their feet firmly in the soil, there would be no need for guns and its amendments, no need to have class discriminations, no need for political parties to raise so much money, and no need for taxes to support them.

By eliminating the desire for present kinds of food, it would also eliminate sex with rape, abortions, kidnapping of children, and jealousy murders. And of course present diseases with so many medical expenses. So simple to solve - if we, like plants would only return to our dependence on the sun, the rain, and the soil for our survival, we could be back in the Garden of Eden at once.

The following are quotes and views of the author:

Judaism expects and demands a greater maturity than many people are ready to accept. It is much easier to reject this degree of maturity by hating the Jews for it

The difference in responsibility is so much greater and stronger that the result even causes many Jews to hate Jews

Life is full of mistakes, misunderstandings and misinformation

When a young child is disappointed in its mother, the child must not show too much anger towards her, (for survival Reasons), so it turns it's anger towards her sister instead, perhaps Just like Islam people who are unhappy, (perhaps with it's government or religion), their rage is turned against others.

The art of being human

1. Learn how to lie
2. Do everything to hurt others
3. Wear lipstick to cover your unclean thoughts and words
4. Blame someone else for your wrongs

What is true can be partially false, and what is false can be partially true

A statement that means actually what is said, can mean the opposite to some people (form of projection), it is what the person wants it to mean.

Stealing people's money is called taxes. Forcing strangers to take care of your children and support them for you is called poverty

The letters that follow, both formal and personal are important to the Author to include in this book. They express her feelings during certain periods and events in her life

You will understand after you have read the letters

Formal Letters

This is my first writing of a page on the Internet.

There is nothing I would like to say that should be put on the screen for people to not understand. I will add more in the future – some things like what I am and am not saying.

New York Post
Editorial Department

July 31, 1990

Answer to
Sheik Wagdi Ghonieon
and his Brooklyn College followers.

I was not aware that I am a descendant of the apes until
you informed me And I am most grateful to you for this
information because until now I never understood why you
hate me so. At last I understand!

I like apes even though I didn't know that I was related to
them. I really like them better than some people

Sincerely,

August 10, 1991

Mr. Thomas Sobol
State Education Department
NY

Dear Mr Sobol:

I understand you are heading a project which I am totally interested in, and I would like to offer my help, salary free.

I am particularly interested in the minority problem, as I have been studying this for twenty years. I would like to know how many minority types are to be studied and which minorities are going to be included and which are going to be excluded.

I am a clinical psychologist (not a historian) and I am offering my help free, under your guidance.

Sincerely yours,

Daily News
New York

Dear Mr. Crouch,

Ref: your August 3, 1997 Article

It is interesting that you mention one single country that is receiving money from U S. You forgot to mention how much Arafat gets, how much Egypt gets, and the others.

If our politicians weren't giving so much to the others, then Israel would not need to accept anything to defend itself and Democracy.

Sincerely, A Devoted Reader

Woody Allen
New York City

Dear Woody,

I love your loudly - heard evaluation of Israel!

I think you are so right, and I hope you will prove it to the world by going there yourself and standing right between the innocent Palestinians and the wicked Israelis, to demonstrate your even-handedness.

In this way you can instantly become the New-World Messiah, and save the world

Sincerely yours,

Mr. Dershowitz
Warner Book

Dear Mr. Dershowitz,

I am particularly interested in the concept of justice, and therefore found your book "Just Revenge" as most important.

I was, however, disappointed in its ending. Your ending would be very pleasing to readers in general, but it is not based on reality. There is just too much evidence that genetic inheritance is not meaningless There can be exceptions where the line of inheritance is stronger or weaker from one source, but it is not eradicated that easily.

I do wonder how you would have ended it if you had not dismissed that fact?

Sincerely yours,

August 23, 2007

Country Division of Planning
Government Center

Dear Sirs:

I have not answered you any sooner because of my pained feelings regarding what was our lifetime homes.

I was forced, by those who give themselves the power, by threats, to remove our buildings. This was in order to protect the neighbor below us and others from injuring themselves when they would break into and steal our possessions

I find it hard to understand why the punishment is for the victim instead of the victimizer. Perhaps you could explain this to me.

Sincerely yours,

September 10, 2007

Kathy Sprague, Town Assessor
New York

Dear Town Assessor,

Instead of protecting us, we were forced by threats to remove our lifetime home buildings in order to protect our neighbor below us from hurting himself when he kept breaking in our buildings to steal our belongings.

Now that taxes still keep increasing, even under such circumstances, can you please tell us how much I am paying extra for the people who call themselves a new "religion" in order not to pay their taxes?

And why have these neighbors been allowed to have their electric poles on our property without our permission?

Sincerely yours,

January 7, 2009

Laurie Dutcher
Tax Collector
NY 14240

Dear Ms Dutcher:

I am enclosing one check for the three separate bills for school taxes.

You have been very kind in responding to me before, and I would so appreciate if you would provide me with some additional information, such as the amount or percentage of my taxes that I am paying for those who do not pay taxes. Perhaps I can feel good knowing the amount of charity I am providing for others

You are most unusual in answering me before and I truly appreciate and honor you for this.

Sincerely yours,

Miami Herald
Executive Editor

Dear Mr. Clifton,

Ref: "The Neighbors" April 1999 "Families Of severely disabled face dilemma over what to give up" by Mireidy Fernandez

The D'Angelos's 25-year old son who is severely disabled, has a day companion and receives 96 diapers each month, but uses six diapers a day. To toilet train him, they had a therapist for six months, and the family had to give that up in favor of more diapers

I would like to recommend a solution for you to give to his constitutionally creative lawyer: Why not have the toilet training therapist spend even a small part of those six months and teach the loving parents, as well as the companion, how to toilet train the son, and even teach the Aunt and Grandparents who all love him?

P S Enclosing copies of your article with pictures.

Sincerely,

Lighthouse for the Blind

Dear Mr. Metcalf:

You will never be forgotten by so many of us.

In this way, you have already attained immortality!

All our love and best wishes,

April 3, 2003

Mr. Alan Nichols, President
Lighthouse for the Blind
Miami, FL

Dear Mr. Nicholas

As a current and long-time member of the Lighthouse for the Blind, I feel the need to involve you as their volunteer President of the Board in a situation that involves an ex-employee, Mr Larry Lawhorn.

It seems that I am the so-called chosen person who does not worry about stating an opinion that is shared by many, and thus, I am taking this opportunity to do just that.

I have the good fortune, or perhaps the misfortune, of being privy to hearing whispered comments from many of the participants expressing their sadness about the loss of Larry Lawhorn and the way he was dismissed

You need to know that people are not happy. The joy we have experienced during our time there with the previous administration, made the Lighthouse a very special place for the clients to feel wanted and cared for.

Larry was responsible for those feelings He is an integral part of creating an atmosphere conducive to the needs of the clients and sometimes beyond their needs. It has turned into a pervasively saddened environment without him there to lend a helping hand and good work. A certain somberness has replaced the contented climate that existed prior to his departure.

We are all feeling devastated and an emptiness for losing Larry. We admired him tremendously for his accomplishments for the Lighthouse He worked seven days a week and long hours He did the networking for the entire Lighthouse and on his own time. He volunteered numerous extra hours and even paid for many extras to save the Lighthouse many thousands of dollars.

The staff, clients, and volunteers are all distraught by such a great loss. It is not easy to maintain a devoted and committed employee, and we feel that the new Director should have more carefully made her decision and perhaps asked the long-time clients for input before making such a destructive decision

On behalf of many of us, please consider bringing Larry Lawhorn back to his previous position at the Lighthouse, where he is much needed and sadly missed.

Sincerely yours,

New York Post
Joyce Brothers

Dear Dr Brothers,

In your column of May 11th in the 'New York Post' referring to the book "Confronting Crime" by Elliot Currie, with which you say you agree, you say inequality of wealth leads to crime.

I would appreciate it if you would clarify this by answering these questions

1. When in our history did we have greater equality?
2. Do you feel that you yourself commit no crimes only because you are not in want?
3. Why is it that so many people who are in want do not commit any crimes?

I would appreciate your comments. I am enclosing a self addressed stamped envelope for a personal reply.

Sincerely yours,

President George W. Bush
The White House

Dear President Bush,

I have no reason to defend anyone except for the obvious purpose of justice or fairness. And since you appear to be really working for justice, which is rare in people of great power, I would like to bring to your attention for examination and correction, without prejudice, which appears to be a lack of justice in relation to the treatment of Pollard vs Robert Hanssen.

I am referring to a documentary shown February 18, 2002 on T V channel A&E about Robert Hanssen, the worst American spy, who was responsible, not only for twenty years of treason, murder of American FBI agents, and other untold harm, He is given even the rights to keep his pension, his home, etc., and is treated with compassion and respect for being a religious man.

In the case of Pollard, he not only never even gave information to an enemy country, but gave information to Israel that had not only been promised to them, but was a promise not being kept, even when it was a serious danger to them from Iraq.

I realize that it is part of human nature, for most people to seek scapegoats in order to make themselves feel and look better. But this never really helps them at all and only creates more injustices in the future, for themselves, as well as for others.

I do not know if you, or anyone else will even read this, but I hope I am mistaken about that, and that somehow I might be informed that you at least heard me. This matter seems to have some similarities to the Dreyfus Affair.

P.S.
I am enclosing corroborating data.

Respectfully yours,

President Bill Clinton
The White House

Dear President Clinton,

You told us that you do not know what "is" is... Personally I find what "is" just is. No matter how I define it

For instance, when death occurs, whether I define it as going to heaven, or being reincarnated, or any of the other definitions - no matter what I call it, or describe it as -I find that it always means that it is. And I have to accept what is, no matter how I try to fool myself. I find it difficult to even fool others, though I say: "He is still here with me."

I do wish you would tell me how I too could make what is to not be, the way you can.

Sincerely,

Note – I received an answer from President Bill Clinton. His answer to me was "he was not going to answer my letter"

August 25, 1999

Dear Sally:

At last I see why lawyers are unable to help me with a justice trust! It is because lawyers are taught not to understand what justice means.

For example, lawyer President Clinton, a Rhodes and Oxford scholar, admitted he doesn't even know what "is" is He suffered such pain from this lack of knowledge that he admitted it before the entire world.

Mr. Jacobowitz sent you the information for which he had charged me $648.80 The information still secret from me, only the charges were not secret. A lawyer's way of thinking? And now you feel it only right that I be expected to pay again for the same information now given to you?

You helped lawyer Saul Feder steal $2,500 from me by generously feeding him unbelievable misinformation which his criminal mind found very useful. Of course, it was not intentional on your part, but does a lawyer's justice mean that I should pay for others' mistakes as well as my own? Is this the meaning of justice?

Sincerely, with love,

National Tax Payers Union
Alexandra, VA
5-24-07

Dear Hopefuls,

Please tell me how you imagine you can possibly accomplish getting the fair tax passed-'-considering the massive I.R.S Federal employees who profit from this unfair mess and would not give it up, nor the endless accountants and lawyers and all their relatives, friends, and their attachments? If you could do this, I would certainly love to help in every way.

Sincerely yours,

Personal Letters

Mr. Herbert Solon
New York City, New York

Dear Mr. Solon:

I keep calling you endlessly and when I do reach you on the phone, you keep repeating that you are taking care of my case against Mr. Sullivan, and you and another lawyer have been working on it, and you keep reminding me that you have paid $60 for serving papers on him and his nephew in October 1972 (to get him to return my money which you had advised and arranged for me to give him in the first place.) You took all my papers then (and you knew I had no copies) and all this time you have been reassuring me over and over that you completed the necessary steps, and that they were served and the SEC was notified and you assured me of success.

You repeatedly told me this on the telephone as well as the times you permitted me to come to your office. You said I would receive corroboration in the mail from you and your other lawyer. When I later reminded you that I had not, and that I still didn't know his name, and couldn't you give me his telephone no. so I could call him? I asked you for something in writing since I had been waiting for over a year. You became defensive and accused me of not trusting you Then, for the first time, you actually said that neither of the men had been served because you didn't believe the nephew was legally responsible (although you were the one who had decided he was) Until now you repeatedly told me that both were responsible and that he was actually served and that the SEC was holding him responsible for causing me to have had to hire another lawyer to get back my money from Mr. Dana to whom you had me pay $2,500 as a retainer fee. Mr. Dana also kept telling me for years that everything was being done but that it takes a great deal of time to get on the calendar, and other fantastic lies. It was only by accident that I learned that I was being deceived by him. It was my dentist whose brother, also a lawyer, had overheard something about what was being done to me, and my dentist told me. (Of course to get my money back by another lawyer – although it was almost instantly – I had to pay an even higher fee)

All these years I never suspected it was you who had my money all those years which you had Mr. Dana pretend that he was the one, and of course my having paid it to him And all those years I never suspected it could be your fault and you kept making me believe it was the fault of Mr. Dana! It was only after your remark that I finally suspected and realized that the money returned to me through hiring a third lawyer, which had been possessed by you for years – and the matter completely and forever neglected – and yet you continued your endless lies over endless telephone calls! All this time this money was yours through Mr Dana, and that Mr. Dana was merely the person who took the money for you.

When I finally realized all the cruel harm you did and the years of hanging me in the air to toss slowly in the air, the thousands of telephone calls you requested from me and the numerous trips to your office – my hurt was so great that I could only respond impotently and therefore unable to do anything. I have been turning my other cheek for so long, and this, and you, are the last straw. You always claimed to be our friend and we trusted and believed you, and you betrayed our every trust and your every word.

Even the money you took for filing a mortgage (You insisted on receiving it in cash but finally agreed to accept part of it by check) Always repeating that you were picking up the mortgage papers for me – and you would keep asking me to call you back endless times, and each time you begged me to wait because you were picking it up that day, the next, and whatever excuse you could make – or someone else was picking it up for you – or had picked it – and always telling me that it was definitely filed. You would imply that I didn't trust you and you would get angry. You even told me that you had picked it up and your papers were somewhere or other, and therefore I couldn't pick it up myself.

And what about all the matters you supposedly did for my husband, and then you always kept that you were supposed to forward to him? I can't imagine what you did with the other people I recommended to you.

And what about the most serious matter of all which involved my sister and her daughter, whose husband Steven Bland was responsible for her being in a coma. You assured us that he and his wealthy family would pay the hospital bills, - and your concern and promises! Until all the witnesses disappeared (we were told the witnesses had been paid off) – and so much later when you returned some of my papers, and there, to our extreme surprise, I found the medical bills that never even been submitted, but had been paid by my husband

It never occur to us that the man of the legal profession would be lying to his client again and again, and on such matters. In retrospect, I can't imagine how I could have been so deceived. I am still the innocent farm girl and stupidly trusting lamb who believed that all people have the integrity and morality that my very poor and completely uneducated farm parents instilled in me

The injuries and intellectual rape you have imprinted upon me are beyond imagination – and in a civilization run by your profession – is far greater than all the monetary losses you were responsible for on our behalf

April 16, 1976

Mr. Oscar J. Cohen
New York City. New York

Dear Mr Cohen –

I received your letter with Mr. Solon's statement and did not answer sooner because I felt so outraged. As you yourself can easily see Since Mr. Solon lied to me about everything while I was his client, it is only natural that he would do no differently for himself.

I am enclosing a copy of the letter I wrote to him on August 1973 from which you can get a picture of some of the things that I know about and have proof. I am enclosing some of the details relating to the matters brought up.

It took me a long time to realize that Mr. Solon is a phychopathic liar, for he appears so kindly and I really thought so well of him

Mr Oscar Cohen   September 30, 1977

Dear Mr. Cohen:

I will try to explain what happened on September 7th. I was assigned by Judge Schwartz to Judge Wolin. I waited in the room where Judge Wolin was to preside.

I noticed that Mr. Solon and Roth were busily coming and going repeatedly After a while Mr. Roth (Mr Solon's attorney) came over to me and said I was to follow him to another room I trustingly followed him and it was not until much later that I realized that I was led to a different judge, arranged by Mr. Roth How else? The judge Mr. Roth took me to was judge Sclar, who at first pretended as if he was helping me because he said to Mr. Solon and Mr. Roth that I needed help because I was undefended Very soon, I realized I was mistakenly naive when none of my evidence was even looked at and instead Judge Sclar just looked down and said to Mr Roth that all this is proof against myself.

I couldn't believe that it was possible for even the worst kind of human being to do and say such a thing and I immediately felt paralyzed by the hopelessness of it all. Then Mr Roth, with a great act of Hollywood showmanship, said to me "Where did you get that manila envelope?" I didn't know what he was referring to and pointed to everything I had for him to show me. He pointed to a folded piece of paper on which I had written some notes and dates about the Geico matter, and accused me of having stolen my papers from

Mr. Solon's office! I expected the judge to inquire about this but he had no intention to do so. I felt so hurt and by such a fantastical extreme trumped up lie, and realizing the judge was set up for this, that after hearing Mr. Solon's lies to questions asked him by the step-up-judge, so that when the judge asked me if I had any questions to ask Mr. Solon, I knew it was all useless, and all I could say was "You will all have to sleep with yourselves while remembering what you have done to me. Judge Sclar dismissed the case. I spoke to Mr Friel, assistant district attorney who advised me to inform you, the bar association and to go to Criminal Court about Mr. Solon's remark about having a bullet put through my head and about Mr. Roth accusing me of stealing my papers.

My problem is that I am afraid that Mr. Solon who claimed to be friendly with some Mafia clients will carry out his threat.

September 1, 1993

Mazel Davis

Dear Mr Davis:

American Savings Bank of Florida has informed me that you have not received my savings book which Gary, manager, has mailed to you because the US post office refuses to deliver your mail when addressed to

East NY Savings Bank
Peter Cooper Branch
East 20 St, and 1st Ave.
N.Y N.Y. 10021?

And that you request a ten dollar fine from me instead of fining the post office for keeping the mail, instead of, at least, returning it to the sender

Now since I <u>don't want another book, and don't need another book</u> for transferring my account, I would like to have an explanation from you that has a iota of rationality to it.

I realize the educators today do not believe in logic, and that logic may not return for at least one or two generations from now. but even if you want to make everything relevant to nothing, I absolutely can not pay for something I don't want and don't need.

So perhaps you can mail some forms for me to sign so that I can withdraw at least part of my money until you bravely contact your post office.

I am enclosing a copy of my receipt from the Am. Savings Bank sent to you about two months ago with my book, etc – which has my account and amount of balance (before interest and direct deposits)

June 14, 1960

Committee on Requirements

Gentlemen:

I wish to thank you for refusing me re-admission to your school. You have thus spared me from further years of fruitless and non-educational "education" in your school.

It was the persistent suggestions of someone in your school that I re-applied for admission. This was in opposition to all my feelings because of the irrationality which I and many others have experienced from your previous faculty and past heads of the school. And at this person's insistence and reassurance of the improvement of your school heads and faculty, I again asked for admission

Now even you consider the previous administration as adequate judges in grading me poorly, and yet, at the same time, you consider them inadequate in admitting me as a PhD student.

This in itself shows me that the irrationality of the school is continuing in the new administration, and such a school can not deserve my respect Thank you for not accepting me

Sincerely yours,

Dear Jean,

I addressed the envelope to you a long time ago but I am finally writing to you today Partly because I get so involved in doing nothing that I forget about the passing of time. But mostly it is that I am so stressed trying to do things, and avoiding doing them, and being frustrated because of it

And it is very hard for me to talk to someone when there is no response - E-mail helps that to some extent because it is so fast. I had a copy of the New York Post yesterday and it has so much more of what I know and am interested in than the local papers - but I hate to pay so much for it down here. I miss so much of the news by not seeing it. In some ways, it is like living in a different country Perhaps you can fill me in on with some of it Looking forward to hearing from you.

PS:
I am enclosing the article about Hillary that I told you about.

Dear Jenny,

I'm not sure I know what you want to know. It would be mainly lab work and usually you get information by different instructors and find out different areas of study that particularly interest you and which is available to you. You have to start somewhere; do you want to be there before you begin?

Your father said you are dissatisfied with the school and that you are lonely. Everyone is lonely when they start somewhere new. What do you expect? The school sounded so wonderful to me. I don't know what the instructors are like, but there must be some that are good.

Do you feel you are not appreciated enough? It is not their purpose to replace parents and friends. If you spend your time really studying hard, you will not be lonely much longer. I promise you that. Let me know what you think your problems are.

Love, Your aunt

Dear Sadye,

Since I have no idea of who or what was said to whom, I feel it is necessary for me to disappear so as not to upset you so. Your resentment toward me goes way back from the beginning of time, and I do not know how to alleviate it.

I do feel saddened by this, but I just have too much to bear without adding this, whatever it is. I have really tried hard to help all the ways I know how Even Shirley-the-Great said to me reproachfully "Why don't you let Philip buy the place? Does Shirley really believe that I have been stopping him? Is that what you believe?

When I told her that Philip has been saying this for months but so far he hasn't. I said to her "I'm not sure how reliable he is because he is disturbed. Shirley answered me angrily "I don't find him disturbed at all". I said: "All right, if he is not disturbed, then it is I who am disturbed It is what she believes and it is apparently what you believe. And so it is and what else can I say?

Dear Sondra,

Misunderstandings occur very easily. I am un-aware of what terrible things I must have said, or if someone else misstated it for me I apologize for whatever I said or didn't say. I do sometimes make satiric remarks, which not everyone understands unless they know me well.

How many Hail Mary's would get your forgiveness? Or what atonement is acceptable?

February 2, 1995

Marcia Bennett - Bernier
New York City, N. Y

Dear Marcia,

I am so sorry to hear about your father. I feel especially pained about it, and for you, because I have had these experiences and more.

Most of this is caused by, or aggravated by, the new definition of democracy that all people are equal, whether competent or not, conscientious or uncaring, good or evil. Many deaths can be attributed to this notion of equality.

I hope things are better for you. Let me know, if I can be of help in any way.

Love,

When you get a chance, please send me the list, that you said you would, of all my additional items that you took – and the prices – so I can have a matching list – before we forget

August 3, 1995

Marcia Bennett - Bernier
New York City, N.Y

Dear Marcia,

Today is my birthday, and it is over 6 months since I wrote
to you, and I haven't heard from you at all. I hope nothing
too troubling has kept you from doing so. As for me – I
would have written sooner again but I have had, and still
have a disturbing family problem that has been making me
crazy, (I've been defrauded of all my assets by a relative, and
I don't want to hurt the rest of the family)

I hope you have better news Please let me know what has
been happening. I hope, especially, that you feel real well

Regards to Alex, I do wish we could have a real long talk.
Remember that you are always welcome where I am.

Love,

March 24, 1996

Marcia Bennett - Bernier
New York City, N. Y

Dear Marcia:

I can't tell you how disappointed and hurt I was that you would not return my calls when I was in New York. I thought you would be pleased to return my unsold things.

I am therefore forced to consider reporting the loss of my merchandise but to be sure I do not incorrectly report what you sold and owe me for, and the things you admit you still have, please send me this information now so I can check off from my lists. I hope you are well and much happier

Love,

April 5, 2000

Marcia Bennett - Bernier
New York City, N. Y

Dear Marcia,

I keep waiting for you to keep your promises, and I am more disappointed than ever. The things that you have admitted to having sold, you still haven't paid me for And you have not returned any of my most valuable items. For instance, whatever you returned I marked off and you only returned some of the paintings but none of the valuable ones. And that applies to everything, that you even bothered to return.

When I speak with someone on the phone, I usually take notes. So when you told me you stopped using my electric bed and folded it up to take up less space, I told you that you could sell it so I could get only $500. And you could keep the rest. And you agreed. This bed has a special motor which never needs repairs of any kind and this bed is not replaceable.

Then when I had a customer for it for you, you suddenly told me that you don't know what happened to it. What would you think if I talked to you like that?

The same thing about the huge quartz – Maybe someone stole it. This quartz was so big and heavy that even the strongest man could not go off with it. And it was a most unusual and beautiful specimen.

All the small and very desirable collectable items, you seem to have lost all records of and all memory of, so you ask me to send you the list and now you have remained silent since you saw the copies in your own handwriting What do you expect me to do? I have always, not only liked you very much, but trusted your honesty, and I was always concerned for your welfare.

I wish you were capable of being more truthful with me. If you wish to pay me for the things you admit to have sold, then I will not include them in the police report.

(P.s... Your boyfriend Alex accidentally admitted to me that he had the bed.)

My best wishes,

Marcia Bennett - Bernier
New York City, N. Y

Dear Marcia,

I still feel sorry for you - knowing that you will have to keep lying to yourself for the rest of your life -to cover your guilt -for stealing all my valued possessions (mine and my parents) knowing bow desperate I was to have to leave everything with you, who pretended to be a friend who could be trusted - all in the hope of saving my hopelessly dying husband

Perhaps you can send me a copy of your dreams?

Marcia Bennett - Bernier
New York City, N. Y

Dear Marcia,

Your mouth kept going, going, going very fast like a guilty war machine. Never stopping from spewing out your factory of lies.

I used to defend you and I used to think you were capable of being a friend, and I couldn't help myself but feel sorrow for what I once thought of as a human being and as a friend.

I always felt kindly toward you, and I couldn't help but feel sorry for you that you should need to prostitute yourself by perjuring yourself in order to steal everything from my family and me

In Memory of you,

Dear Olga,

You are poisoning yourself with your thoughts. Instead of thinking of how you can solve each problem, you think how someone is at fault in not doing it for you

You keep reminding yourself constantly what and how someone else did it wrong, and especially how someone did it wrong only to you and against you.

This is the way you are poisoning yourself and it is the way to drive yourself mad, and that is the way mad becomes crazy.

You get mad when someone else doesn't know, or do, everything, but you don't think you are supposed to do or know everything. You forget that everyone is as human as you are.

You get mad when, something is not immediate for you, but no cure is immediate except death

You get mad_____

You get mad_____

You get mad_____

You get mad_____

You can list all the things you are mad about, including me and everyone and everything, and then let us talk about it.

Love,

Personal Letters

August 24, 1973

Dear Mr. Solon

I keep calling you endlessly and when I do reach you on the phone, you keep repeating that you are taking care of my case against Mr. Sullivan, and you and another lawyer have been working on it, and you keep reminding me that you have paid $60 for serving papers on him and his nephew in October 1972 (to get him to return my money which you had advised and arranged for me to give him in the first place) You took all my papers then (and you knew I had no copies) and all this time you have been reassuring me over and over that you completed the necessary steps, and that they were served and the SEC was notified and you assured me of success.

You repeatedly told me this on the telephone as well as the times you permitted me to come to your office. You said I would receive corroboration in the mail from you and your other lawyer. When I later reminded you that I had not, and that I still didn't know his name, and couldn't you give me his telephone no. so I could call him? I asked you for something in writing since I had been waiting for over a year. You became defensive and accused me of not trusting you Then, for the first time, you actually said that neither of the men had been served because you didn't believe the nephew was legally responsible (although you were the one who had decided he was) Until now you repeatedly told me that both were responsible and that he was actually served and that the SEC was holding him responsible for causing me to have had to hire another lawyer to get back my money from Mr Dana to whom you had me pay $2,500 as a retainer fee. Mr. Dana also kept telling me for years that everything was being done but that it takes a great deal of time to get on the calendar, and other fantastic lies. It was only by accident that I learned that I was being deceived by him It was my dentist whose brother, also a lawyer, had overheard something about what was being done to me, and my dentist told me (Of course to get my money back by another lawyer – although it was almost instantly – I had to pay an even higher fee.)

All these years I never suspected it was you who had my money all those years which you had Mr. Dana pretend that he was the one, and of course my having paid it to him. And all those years I never suspected it could be your fault and you kept making me believe it was the fault of Mr. Dana! It was only after your remark that I finally suspected and realized that the money returned to me through hiring a third lawyer, which had been possessed by you for years – and the matter completely and forever neglected – and yet you continued your endless lies over endless telephone calls!

All this time this money was yours through Mr Dana, and that Mr. Dana was merely the person who took the money for you.

When I finally realized all the cruel harm you did and the years of hanging me in the air to toss slowly in the air, the thousands of telephone calls you requested from me and the numerous trips to your office – my hurt was so great that I could only respond impotently and therefore unable to do anything. I have been turning my other cheek for so long, and this, and you, are the last straw You always claimed to be our friend and we trusted and believed you, and you betrayed our every trust and your every word.

Even the money you took for filing a mortgage (You insisted on receiving it in cash but finally agreed to accept part of it by check.) Always repeating that you were picking up the mortgage papers for me – and you would keep asking me to call you back endless times, and each time you begged me to wait because you were picking it up that day, the next, and whatever excuse you could make – or someone else was picking it up for you – or had picked it – and always telling me that it was definitely filed. You would imply that I didn't trust you and you would get angry. You even told me that you had picked it up and your papers were somewhere or other, and therefore I couldn't pick it up myself.

And what about all the matters you supposedly did for my husband, and then you always kept what you were supposed to forward to him? I can't imagine what you did with the other people I recommended to you.

And what about the most serious matter of all which involved my sister and her daughter, whose husband Steven Bland was responsible for her being in a coma. You assured us that he and his wealthy family would pay the hospital bills, - and your concern and promises! Until all the witnesses disappeared (we were told the witnesses had been paid off) – and so much later when you returned some of my papers, and there, to our extreme surprise, I found the medical bills that had never even been submitted, but had been paid by my husband.

It never occured to us that the man of the legal profession would be lying to his client again and again, and on such matters. In retrospect, I can't imagine how I could have been so deceived. I am still the innocent farm girl and stupidly trusting lamb who believed that all people have the integrity and morality that my very poor and completely uneducated farm parents instilled in me.

The injuries and intellectual rape you have imprinted upon me are beyond imagination – and in a civilization run by your profession – is far greater than all the monetary losses you were responsible for on our behalf

April 16, 1976

Dear Mr. Cohen –

I received your letter with Mr. Solon's statement and did not answer sooner because I felt so outraged. As you yourself can easily see. Since Mr Solon lied to me about everything while I was his client, it is only natural that he would do no differently for himself.

I am enclosing a copy of the letter I wrote to him on August 1973 from which you can get a picture of some of the things that I know about and have proof I am enclosing some of the details relating to the matters brought up.

It took me a long time to realize that Mr. Solon is a phychopathic liar, for he appears so kindly and I really thought so well of him

September 30, 1977

Dear Mr. Cohen:

I will try to explain what happened on September 7th. I was assigned by Judge Schwartz to Judge Wolin I waited in the room where Judge Wolin was to preside

I noticed that Mr. Solon and Roth were busily coming and going repeatedly. After a while Mr. Roth (Mr. Solon's attorney) came over to me and said I was to follow him to another room. I trustingly followed him and it was not until much later that I realized that I was led to a different judge, arranged by Mr. Roth How else? The judge Mr. Roth took me to was judge Sclar, who at first pretended as if he was helping me because he said to Mr. Solon and Mr. Roth that I needed help because I was undefended. Very soon, I realized I was mistakenly naïve when none of my evidence was even looked at and instead Judge Sclar just looked down and said to Mr. Roth that all this is proof against myself.

I couldn't believe that it was possible for even the worst kind of human being to do and say such a thing and I immediately felt paralyzed by the hopelessness of it all. Then Mr. Roth, with a great act of Hollywood showmanship, said to me "Where did you get that manila envelope?" I didn't know what he was referring to and pointed to everything I had for him to show me He pointed to a folded piece of paper on which I had written some notes and dates about the Geico matter, and accused me of having stolen my papers from

Mr. Solon's office! I expected the judge to inquire about this but he had no intention to do so. I felt so hurt and by such a fantastical extreme trumped up lie, and realizing the judge was set up for this, that after hearing Mr. Solon's lies to questions asked him by the step-up-judge, so that when the judge asked me if I had any questions to ask Mr. Solon, I knew it was all useless, and all I could say was "You will all have to sleep with yourselves while remembering what you have done to me.: Judge Sclar dismissed the case. I spoke to Mr Friel, assistant district attorney who advised me to inform you, the bar association and to go to Criminal Court about Mr. Solon's remark about having a bullet put through my head and about Mr Roth accusing me of stealing my papers.

My problem is that I am afraid that Mr. Solon who claimed to be friendly with some Mafia clients will carry out his threat.

September 1, 1993

Mazel Davis
East NY Savings Bank
New York, NY

Dear Mr Davis:

American Savings Bank of Florida has informed me that you have not received my savings book which Gary, manager, has mailed to you because the US post office refuses to deliver your mail when addressed to
East NY Savings
Branch
N Y. N.Y. 10021?

And that you request a ten dollar fine from me instead of fining the post office for keeping the mail, instead of, at least, returning it to the sender

Now since I <u>don't want another book, and don't need another book</u> for transferring my account, I would like to have an explanation from you that has a iota of rationality to it.

I realize the educators today do not believe in logic, and that logic may not return for at least one or two generations from now... but even if you want to make everything relevant to nothing, I absolutely can not pay for something I don't want and don't need.

So perhaps you can mail some forms for me to sign so that I can withdraw at least part of my money until you bravely contact your post office

I am enclosing a copy of my receipt from the Am Savings Bank sent to you about two months ago with my book, etc – which has my account and amount of balance (before interest and direct deposits).

June 14, 1960

Committee on Requirements
New School for Social Research

Gentlemen:

I wish to thank you for refusing me re-admission to your school You have thus spared me from further years of fruitless and non-educational "education" in your school.

It was the persistent suggestions of someone in your school that I re-applied for admission. This was in opposition to all my feelings because of the irrationality which I and many others have experienced from your previous faculty and past heads of the school. And at this person's insistence and reassurance of the improvement of your school heads and faculty, I again asked for admission

Now even you consider the previous administration as adequate judges in grading me poorly, and yet, at the same time, you consider them inadequate in admitting me as a PhD student.

This in itself shows me that the irrationality of the school is continuing in the new administration, and such a school can not deserve my respect. Thank you for not accepting me.

Sincerely yours,

Dear Jean,

I addressed the envelope to you a long time ago but I am finally writing to you today. Partly because I get so involved in doing nothing that I forget about the passing of time But mostly it is that I am so stressed trying to do things, and avoiding doing them, and being frustrated because of it.

And it is very hard for me to talk to someone when there is no response - E-mail helps that to some extent because it is so fast. I had a copy of the New York Post yesterday and it has so much more of what I know and am interested in than the local papers - but I hate to pay so much for it down here. I miss so much of the news by not seeing it In some ways, it is like living in a different country. Perhaps you can fill me in on with some of it. Looking forward to hearing from you.

PS:
I am enclosing the article about Hillary that I told you about

Dear Jenny,

I'm not sure I know what you want to know. It would be mainly lab work and usually you get information in different instructors and find out different areas of study that particularly interest you and which is available to you. You have to start somewhere; do you want to be there before you begin?

Your father said you are dissatisfied with the school and that you are lonely. Everyone is lonely when they start somewhere new. What do you expect? The school sounded so wonderful to me. I don't know what the instructors are like, but there must be some that are good.

Do you feel you are not appreciated enough? It is not their purpose to replace parents and friends. If you spend your time really studying hard, you will not be lonely much longer I promise you that Let me know what you think your problems are.
Love, Your aunt

Dear Sadye,

Since I have no idea of who or what was said to whom, I feel it is necessary for me to disappear so as not to upset you so Your resentment toward me goes way back from the beginning of time, and I do not know how to alleviate it.

I do feel saddened by this, but I just have too much to bear without adding this, whatever it is. I have really tried hard to help all the ways I know how Even Shirley-the-Great said to me reproachfully "Why don't you let Philip buy the place? Does Shirley really believe that I have been stopping him? Is that what you believe?

When I told her that Philip has been saying this for months but so far he hasn't I said to her "I'm not sure how reliable he is because he is disturbed. Shirley answered me angrily "I don't find him disturbed at all". I said: "All right, if he is not disturbed, then it is I who am disturbed. It is what she believes and it is apparently what you believe And so it is and what else can I say?

Dear Sondra,

Misunderstandings occur very easily. I am un-aware of what terrible things I must have said, or if someone else misstated it for me. I apologize for whatever I said or didn't say. I do sometimes make satiric remarks, which not everyone understands unless they know me well.

How many Hail Mary's would get your forgiveness? Or what atonement is acceptable?

Dear Olga,

You are poisoning yourself with your thoughts. Instead of thinking of how you can solve each problem, you think how someone is at fault in not doing it for you

You keep reminding yourself constantly what and how someone else did it wrong, and especially how someone did it wrong only to you and against you.

This is the way you are poisoning yourself and it is the way to drive yourself mad, and that is the way mad becomes crazy.

You get mad when someone else doesn't know, or do, everything, but you don't think you are supposed to do or know everything. You forget that everyone is as human as you are.

You get mad when, something is not immediate for you, but no cure is immediate except death

You get mad_____
You get mad_____
You get mad_____
You get mad_____

You can list all the things you are mad about, including me and everyone and everything, and then let us talk about it.

Love,

To The Town –

Our property that our parent's purchased unseen because they couldn't afford more had been owned by American Indians.

People came to get water on the property and called it "Long Leban Vaser".

There was (and is) their burial grounds which my Mother did not permit me to dig up. Which I wanted to do so much. There is a cave up on the hill where there are Indian drawings and objects on the walls.

And now, the amount being used for those you do not pay taxes added on to the amount I was forced to pay with the threat of confiscation of my property and forced to remove all our life-long family buildings in order to protect a neighbor who kept breaking in to steal our stoves, refrigerators and antique furniture and belongings, to protect him in case he got hurt while doing this.

Introduction

Mother Hen

She called herself the mother hen She decided what is her table, her house.

She felt good about this and was very proud and wanted everybody to know how good she was because she was the mother hen

She chose everything first for herself and her decisions were the only correct ones, correct for everyone of course.

Yes, everything had to be her way and if anything was not so, the other person had to be very guilty

She watched her table for a chick to disobey and that chick got a barage of accusations added to the actual one.

Yes, she was a real mother hen the same way I experienced it on the farm.

The mother hen would take the baby chicks under her wings, but when a chick was injured, the mother hen would peck at the injured chick until the chick was dead.

As a small child my mother would have me take care of an injured chick to keep it away from its mother until the injury was healed before it could be safely returned to its mother hen.

This human mother hen said to the injured chick (that's me): "You can't sit at my table anymore."

This chick felt it was her own fault for not having left before. She said to mother hen: "Ok" but wanted to also say: "Thank you for freeing me from your control, and giving me back my freedom."

So you can now see the similarity of this mother hen and the nature of mother hens.

The Cricket Guest

I didn't know that crickets came with smoke detectors. My live-in cricket actually came later, but I'll never know when, because they both seemed to have the exact same pitch and both usually made these short chirp-like sounds.

Before I discovered I had the cricket as a guest in my home, I used to wonder why the smoke detector went off while I was sleeping. I would get out of bed and check the stove and hallway for fire.

I knew that it lived with me, I couldn't always tell, though for the last two or more months, my cricket felt safe enough to chirp almost constantly.

It stayed within the vicinity of the smoke detector but sometimes traveled to other areas. I had never seen him but must have come close to touching him when I heard him moving on my desk as I was about to turn on a lamp there. In fact, he sounded only inches away as I was typing

It was not until I actually saw one near my lamp that made me really sure of his existence. At times he seemed to chirp almost constantly. Though I was glad he was there. I actually feared touching him or even seeing him in this inappropriate environment – knowing what crickets look like Before seeing it, I sometimes heard movements on my desk, and it would scare me. They looked like dried skeletons on tall straw legs. I was also afraid I might kill it by mistake since they were hardly seeable and didn't seem to have any body at all

Several people, who heard him and discovered his identity, asked me what I feed him. While I was surprised by this question, I wondered if I was starving him. I opened the terrace door often enough to free him if he needed to, or wanted to leave, but it seemed he wanted to be out of the cold

While we only saw one, for all I know, the cricket may not have been alone, because they would not be recognizable to me when not together. Perhaps when there was constant chirping, it was his conversation with others present or elsewhere, and they may even be hatching a slew of themselves, for that is probably what crickets do.

Later on, the cricket had been singing beautiful songs at times, perhaps in anticipation of spring mating. When later I couldn't hear him at all and was concerned that his lifespan was up, I felt it as a loss

However, one night I heard him cheerfully chirp away and it brightened up everything again for me

But President Reagan's wife, according to a newspaper article, had a similar visitor in the White House, and she felt afraid too, as I did, but she said that she had arranged for its removal.

What do you think was strange about this? That a cricket landed in a city apartment on the seventh floor and was competing with smoke detector?

Not me. What was unbelievable to me was that I could feel guilty about a cricket, and that I felt deserted when I thought it was gone.

A Soul Sings Inside

About my cricket, it still lived with me later on. People I knew did not understand why I did not want to eliminate its existence - just the way our First Lady did at the White House.

They see my appreciation of a cricket as something wrong with me. Like I was so lonely that I needed a cricket. It was not that I didn't know loneliness but more that the people I knew did not understand me.

One day a man who was doing some repairs in my apartment heard the cricket and he did understand somewhat. He said to me: "It is like having the country inside the city."

Yes it was, but it was also more than that - yes, related to nature and the country - it was that a little ugly bug that could sing like that - for me it had a little bit of whatever god might be, in it.

One day last fall as I walked along with a neighbor Anne. I picked up one of the colorful leaves.

She said to me kindly: "What do you need it for? What are you going to do with it?" I said: "I'm not going to do anything with it; It's just so beautiful."

But to her it was a kind of garbage picking.

Unconditional Love (Found At Last)

Marilyn said to me: "I have finally found unconditional love."

She said: "Isn't it a fact that roaches run away from people? That's what it used to be with me."

"But lately they come to me. They come from out of hiding and run right into my arms"

Even as I waited on line at the supermarket, a girl next to her watched as a cockroach on the counter, ran toward her and onto her arm

The cashier too said she never saw anything like that before. The cashier, though pleasantly surprised, helped the customer reject this loving gesture.

Thus Marylyn has finally discovered true unconditional love, if not by a man, then by a man's ancestor

A Summer day in Manhattan

The weather was so cheerful that it made Ruth feel better as she walked briskly toward the station She was pleased with herself for getting up while everyone else was still asleep But at the same time, she felt sorry for herself, because she, too, might have slept late, as it was Thanksgiving Day

It would take her at least four hours to travel back and forth from Croton to New York City and pick up her altered dress. But it was that important Even her dressmaker had opened especially for her.

Ruth couldn't bear to let Hubert see her again in anything she had worn before. Her fiancé felt displeased enough with her, as it was. This was a black, sleek, sophisticated dress that revealed her to advantage, the kind Hubert always admired on other girls. This dress, she thought, might help her start all over again with him on their Thanksgiving date.

Settling herself on the empty train, Ruth felt lonely. Except for some railroad men, everyone seemed to be staying home today. She let her mind drift back to the subject that obsessed her these days As she thought of the way Hubert sometimes looked at her, it made her collapse within herself and she sank lower into her seat. Even worse were the times when he would look at her, yet not see her at all. Painfully, she remembered everything in detail that she had worn for him and all the different ways she had tried to look to please him. Disappointments were associated in her mind with everything she wore

Ruth found the same deserted loneliness in the city, on the subway, and on the streets. She was satisfied, however, that she had come, for her trip was successful. She left the little shop hugging her package to her, feeling secure and confident. Hubert couldn't help but notice her in this new dress. She pictured him with his eyes sparkling as they used to when he told her endearing things

She was beautiful and brilliant when he used to think so But now that he noticed everything wrong with her, she couldn't help but do everything wrong Somehow she couldn't carry herself the way she used to Parts of her body just didn't work together

She often spoke the opposite of what she intended to say Her thinking was not clear, and she could hardly control her emotions when she meant so much to be pleasant and gay. At times she felt herself cringing, and often she recognized a tinge of begging voice.

These emotions seemed foreign to her, for they jumped unbidden into the open out of unknown recesses. She did not like herself for having them, and it made her feel all the worse.

Ruth got to the subway without having been aware of walking there She was aroused into awareness by the feel of mobs on the street. And then she saw them.

The streets were filled with people, people who were full of longing for new things and new experiences. Most of the people were living through the interests of their children. Today was Macy's Thanksgiving Day Parade, and they were taking the excited children out for a happy afternoon.

Children were everywhere. Parents held some in their arms and others by the hand Every child had a balloon as part of the celebration. All the balloons were alike, except that some were blue and some red All were attached to long sharp sticks.

Trainmen guarded the outer entrance of the sub-way station to keep everyone out. The trains could not accommodate the crowds The unusual influx of people was met with an even greater scarcity of trains due to the current fuel strike.

Ruth waited for thirty minutes in the tightly packed crowd at the subway entrance Squashed and squirming frustrated children only heightened Ruth's tense anxiety to get home Balloons moved unexpectedly toward her from every direction.

At last a train was arriving and the doors opened! She shoved her way through, thinking only of getting back to Hubert. Clutching her token desperately, she finally got near a turnstile only to hear a guard shouting. "No downtown trains! Only uptown trains at this station today."

Frantically she pushed her way out and tried to hail a taxi Time was passing! No empty taxis!

The bus, packed to bursting, would not stop. After twenty minutes of rushing about wildly, she forced her way into a stuffed bus. Children took up extra space as they wriggled about. The bus crawled down the avenue.

Wrapped up in her own anxiety, Ruth only half heard parents begging their children to keep quiet while they cried for seats and attention.

They screamed and jumped for their balloons, as parents tried to hold them up high out of passengers' eyes.

Forty-five minutes later, Ruth got to the street, irritable and nervous, but she still had to make her way eastward. Empty taxis apparently didn't run on the avenue. Precious time was passing!

She had already missed two trains, and if she did not make this one, Hubert surely wouldn't wait. At last a crosstown bus stopped. But trucks kept getting in the way, as if conspiring to keep her from getting to the station. If only there were no traffic lights!

It took people forever to get in and out of the bus The children kept dragging behind with their balloons catching onto everything. The avenue! If only she could get to the next avenue, she'd take the shuttle to Grand Central Station. That might save time

The bus just sat and did not move Two minutes! Three minutes! Anything would be better than this standing still.

The nervousness of the people around her made her even more jittery

Unable to stand it any longer, Ruth jumped out of the car and raced through the streets, startling the children and upsetting their balloons as she reached the shuttle entrance

Arriving at Grand Central, Ruth found it mobbed with holiday travellers She ran, pushing through them, her hair limp, clothes dragging, and feet swollen. Breathlessly, she forced her way past the conductor, who was already closing the gate.

Clutching her package, untied and shabby, she sank into a seat. The excitement had been too much for her But her hiccups stopped suddenly when the conductor said, "You have the wrong train The next stop is where you are going."

Ruth couldn't understand her feelings. For strangely, she felt relieved. It was better this way, for Hubert would never be satisfied.

As always she had done the best she could. But with him, it would always be considered the wrong thing.

Feeling free for the first time in four years, she straightened up in her seat, and comfortably and happily gazed out of the window

Like An African Queen

She was very tall and stately. Though not young, she moved like an African Queen. I watched her walk with admiration as I crossed behind her.

She wore a long dress and a draped kerchief on her head She suddenly stopped in front of me, and arranging herself by degrees, she pushed her dress way up with graceful competence, and there, with legs wide apart, her dress well draped, and with no undergarments to restrain her, remaining very gracefully upright and head high, she urinated in the center of the sidewalk, strongly and for a long time

She urinated right in the middle of the wide triangular sidewalk in the midst of crisscross traffic, on Broadway.

Although she exposed herself all the way, she showed no concern or embarrassment. For me, dusk and the blackness of her body aided my embarrassed fascination.

Then draping her long skirt back in place, she walked on as before, as queenly as could be.

Nrogi And The Scapegoat

We were friendly and helpful in our working proximity for several years until he became concerned about political problems in his native Africa

He then kept badgering me about my lack of concern about this. I finally asked him if he expected me to go to Africa and fight there for him, while he remained here in the United States?

I purchased a huge button with the word "Scapegoat" across it and wrote my own name on the top and his name, (after the word "for") under it, and wore it for him to see After a while he realized somewhat what he was doing, blaming me for his own anger and guilt.

But soon his wife left him after he explained to his maturing daughter that where he came from, it is permissible to have sex with the father

Do Women Talk Too Much?

I was returning from a late evening class and a woman and three men got on the bus at 34th. The woman said: "A man is beating up a woman and there is no policeman." One of the men had a whistle and he blew it but still there was no sign of a policeman.

She kept on saying. "What a shame it is I don't care what she did he has no right to beat her. No One before seemed to think it was their business to interfere and they decided that the woman must have done something to deserve it." She kept repeating it over and over again.

I was sitting in front of the bus and I said to the driver "Why not stop there and see what is happening?" He agreed to stop and some passengers rushed up to the front of the bus to see.

The bus driver honked his horn as he drove closer. The crying woman was a big blond, hysterical and unable to defend herself. She ran into the street among the moving cars, and finally, when the light turned red, she got into a cab, but with the man running after her. The people in the bus screamed for the taxi not to let him in, but of course he couldn't hear and the taxi rode on with both of them inside. The man continued to hit the woman

The bus driver gave chase after the taxi and kept honking his horn. The woman in our bus said someone should beat him up The bus driver opened his door and the three men ran out

The taxi stopped and the woman ran out with the man after her. The three men knocked the man down. The bus driver then drove off and the women passengers went back to their seats. This time the woman had not talked too much.

To The Town –

Our property that our parent's purchased unseen because they couldn't afford more had been owned by American Indians.

People came to get water on the property and called it "Long Leban Vaser"

There was (and is) their burial grounds which my Mother did not permit me to dig up. Which I wanted to do so much. There is a cave up on the hill where there are Indian drawings and objects on the walls.

And now, the amount being used for those you do not pay taxes added on to the amount I was forced to pay with the threat of confiscation of my property and forced to remove all our life-long family buildings in order to protect a neighbor who kept breaking in to steal our stoves, refrigerators and antique furniture and belongings, to protect him in case he got hurt while doing this.

Esther, The Internationally acclaimed Pianist

Esther complained to me that she can't sleep and asked me to come with her to see a play As soon as we sat down in the theatre she was asleep.

Before leaving with Esther, my husband asked me what we were seeing. "Esther goes there to sleep, I told him, and even if she's awake she never understands it, unless it is music." Esther gets angry if the story doesn't agree with her ideas, and she wants to teach everyone the correct way that she sees it.

Esther had told me that she saw the English movie 'The Chariot" which she liked. She said the runner thought they didn't want him to run because of their anti-Semitism, but that it was only in his own mind. "The writer didn't think so," I told her.

When we got to the theatre, I found out that we were to see two musicals, the second one about Mayor Koch.

Before the play began, Esther was immediately asleep in her seat. She looked very comfortable there, as if it were her natural sleeping position. The first musical did not wake her. She slept on to the end of it and through the long intermission.

The second musical "How you are doing, Eddie?" started and she was still asleep. The screaming did not wake her As the Mayor screamed on the stage, Esther snored, and since she insists on sitting up front, I pressed her arm, she stopped the snores for a while, but she slept on.

The screams across the stage from the balcony did not wake her. The screams of the bag lady did not wake her. The screaming across the stage did not wake her. Again the screaming from the opposite side of the stage from the top of the balcony did not wake her. The screaming back and forth from the back to front and back again did not wake her.

At the last screaming from the entire cast Esther raised her head but her eyes remained closed. Then her head went down again

The loud applause did not wake her It was now 3 1/2 hours that she had slept. The lights went on and she awoke and said to me: "I slept through the whole thing." "Don't I know it?" I said As we left she said: "It's too early to go home I won't be able to sleep so early."

"Where did you get the flowers? Esther asked me. They were particularly beautiful and I had placed them in the kitchen in two places, because it is the place where I spend most of my time when I return from work. "Would you like some? I asked in answer "You couldn't pay me to have flowers in the house," she answered. I had some on the piano and it cost me $800 to repair it when the water from the flowers got into the piano."

"You don't have to have them on the piano." "Where should I keep them, in the kitchen like you? That's no place for flowers; the only place to show them off is on the piano. I will never have flowers in the house again" she said.

In 1920 Esther was eleven years old, and with her father, her pregnant mother, and her two-year old brother left Odessa, Russia, on a freight train.

They were permitted to get transportation by claiming they were going to their hometown near the border. They were running away, and the thing to do was to get as far away as they could to another country. They had to bring with them necessities, including a chamber pot.

When they got off at the border they had to walk to the shoreline - which had extremely sharp declines, both up and down. They had to hire two husky men to help them.

They then had to wait for midnight because the men were in the transport business illegally. They would often murder the people to steal all their belongings In this case they took the family, but said they could not take Esther on the first trip and would have to return for her.

What happened to her before she finally met with her family she could not easily talk about and would sometimes deny or change her story. But the abandonment and experience was forever marked deeply within her.

This she carried with her during all her musical acclaim, and of course it colored all her remarkable abilities and peculiarities - and was beyond reach for her to free herself from it.

The family had to flee Russia at the time because all who were considered capitalists were being annihilated - murdered - and, though her father was not considered to be a capitalist, not having any employees, he was next to that because he was involved in exporting or importing.

Under these circumstances, one would imagine that Esther would be passionate against Communism, but instead her nostalgia for those years before her traumatic experiences are much stronger

Esther, though fleeing with her family for their lives, from Communism - yet wishes for an American kind of Communism

The Neighbor And Food Stamps

A woman in the neighborhood telephoned to tell me about her inability to walk much because of a fall. She went on to say she had trouble doing her shopping. "Can't one of your friends in the building help you?" "No, I have trouble getting anyone," she said.

Thinking she might be starving, I agreed to help her, though I live more than fifteen blocks away, and hardly know her.

She gave me her order consisting of two dozen cans of cat food, which had to be purchased at a particular store at a particular price.

Then she described at which other store I was to go for her grapefruits, how many and at what price. And at another more distant store for the fish and the number of slices to be cut, etc.

Since I had already agreed to do so, I held my displeasure in check Then she told me to first pick up her food stamps.

When I asked her how and where could I possibly do that? "Don't you know?" she answered.

"No," I said. "You mean you don't get food stamps! Everybody gets food stamps" "Everyone?" I asked: "Everyone I know; everyone living around here," she said.

Well, I did her shopping the way she specified, but I never learned how to pick up her food stamps.

Sometimes Anybody Can Be Somebody

I tried and tried to turn on my TV but nothing came on.

Finally, I called customer service to tell them and they told me that I should ask anybody and anybody would turn it on for me - just anybody - could turn it on.

The next morning, I still did not have anybody, so I expressed my desperation to somebody and somebody did send me anybody.

This anybody tried everything he could think of, but it still did not work So he suggested that somebody could do what this anybody could not do.

Sadly, this anybody was feeling like a nobody, yet he did continue to try, as anybody would and like anybody, he suddenly turned it on.

Now, he felt that he had suddenly become a somebody and was no longer an anybody.

Since then, when he passes me, he greets me with open arms, as if I were responsible for his discovering the somebody within himself and was no longer anybody.

Poems

I Think Of Silence

I think of silence when my nerves are infected with the hyperactivity of jiggling music.

I think of silence when I am imprisoned in the violent noises of our underground dungeons, the subways.

Most of all I think of the vow of silence as the only possible therapy for friendly acquaintances, who gift me with their endless circular (circuitous) talk that never stops.

Times Square

The lights twinkle their stars into your soul and
Twinkle them out through your eyes.
They wrap you in jewels, and follow you
Breathing with your movements
And rhyming with your heart

I See Teachers As Students In New York

Teachers, teachers everywhere
And not a thought to think
Teachers, teachers everywhere
Over methods we make a stink.

What if we had an idea, a thought - do you suppose -
Would happen to our methods bought
At twenty dollars a point, in diplomas sealed?
New ways would automatically grow
And leave behind this dirth congealed?

Oh water, water everywhere
We need to wash this teaching profession
And make of all its preaching air
A non- prostituted confession

Why do teachers cheat and lie
When teachers become students in this college?
For fortune they must show their grades of courage
Bandaged round these marks to show
How many friends their papers owe.

Frightened pupils they become when they their teaching
Masks do drop - filled with authoritarian steel
Their veins in stiffness must they hold
To prove their ability to mark and fold
Compulsives act to keep themselves from seeing
What uselessness to society they make of beings.

Farewell, farewell, but this I tell
We need to wash this teaching profession
He prayeth well who loveth well
A non-prostituted confession

Money Honey

I can't give you anything but money
Love is unfit for human-kind
There's no new world paved with love to find
For all this world seemingly so sunny.

Every maiden yet cries out for love
Goes through life picking of its flowers
Always seeking something that's above
instead of picturing greenbacks in her bowers.

The world's as old as money, tis true, let's not forsake it
Romance, youth and love wither and die
Let's abide it, it is so much more clever
To fall in love with money, that goes on forever and ever

Youth and love wither and die, romantic
Love's paved with poets' anguish, gripping, frantic
There's no new world paved with honey

No, our new world has not been paved with love Our brave
new world still finds that love is blind So I can't give you
anything but money, Honey Love is not something fit for
us to find

Still all the world cries out for love, for love
Yet it is money there're thinking of
Instead of love, foolish foolish little flowers
Can't they picture greenbacks in their bowers?

Our world has grown old with money
Youth and love wither and die, funny

But age goes on forever ever
Let us abide, it is much more clever
To just fall in love with money, forever
Money, Honey, Funny, ever and ever.

It's The System

Do you know who's to blame? Not you, not me, It's the System!
THE TERRIBLE, TERRIBLE SYSTEM

If I do bad, it's the fault of the System;
But if I do good, it's never the System.

If I don't have enough to eat, it's the fault of the System
If I eat too much, is it the System?

If you're going to tell me it's my responsibility,
I can just smile and say, "No, it's the System"
THE TERRIBLE, TERRIBLE SYSTEM

Don't tell on me, and I won't tell on you
Remember, we have the System. So let's call everything
the System
THE TERRIBLE, TERRIBLE SYSTEM

Who me? No never me.
Not you or me. It's the System!

I Hold My Breath

I hold my breath when I am told I should be like everyone.

I hold my breath when I am asked for my opinion that is not even heard or listened to.

I hold my breath when people quote me so inaccurately that it is hopeless to try and correct it.

I hold my breath when people attribute to me what they themselves want to believe.

I hold my breath when I hear demands and criticisms of others, which are unfair

I hold my breath when I feel harangued by empty repetitious opinions.

I hold my breath when I say, "You are right" to help someone stop from continuing to say what is not right

I hold my breath, and suffer the consequences, even more - from holding my breath.

I start to breath when I distance myself enough to observe and realize that all people are what they are, just as I am what I am, and try to understand.

Alone

We Are Alone, As Jesus Was
Deserted By All, As Jesus Was

Morality and Justice Are
Equated with Oil
Now it's Oil, Oil, Oil

We are Again
Alone, Alone, Alone
As Jesus Was

The Heavens

Life stretched itself over a mountain, touched hands with the stars, and threw them over the heavens. It picked up the planets and with strings around their centers, tied them all around the moon, causing the moon to fly wildly and ecstatically over the skies

Then to calm them, life slapped its hands against the waters of the sun. Below a fierce streak of fire struck through the skies. It struck through the elements that had previously risen proudly through the skies.

The trees blew ice all over the smoke, but the fire climbed the skies while walking the earth into the tunnels. The windows of the world crashed, and the panes flew by the birds onto a fountain of blood.

The fire curled around the forests and dug life into the ground. The heavens in turn curled themselves over the black smoke and fought hard for the keys of the kingdom

Truth danced and cried for the life that had fallen through. The torn pages of life were now walking the floors of the sky. Madness was tipping its red false hats to the sun.

The sun and the stars then held hands and cried for the truth that had fallen down into the mud. The lights went out but something flew over the trees and played music over the whisperings of the moon.

Afterword

Kitten On The Roof

It's no fun being a kitten; they shove me out here on the roof so I won't dirty the house It's not my fault they can't train me.

I want more attention. I haven't been petted and fed for hours. Perhaps if I press my face against the glass, someone will open that blue French window. Meow. Meow I'll try louder. Meow. Meow. Meow I'm disappointed, but I'll try the other window. I'll try a quick start up that slope. I had better keep running, it is easier that way.

When I run this fast, I get invigorated by the scented breeze and forget to be mad. It makes me feel I am running right up over the green tree-tops into the blue ocean of sky, but the big shiny sun ball gets in my way

I forget about food when I play with these crisp orange, green, yellow, and brown leaves. They crunch when I tap them with my paw. I push them, and as they slide along, I lunge to chase them, sometimes hitting them too hard and they are no longer curled.

The mounds of dried pine needles are fun too when the wind blows them around. I like to run after things as they move I try to catch the flies as they zigzag around me I would swallow them, but they are too fast for me.

This splintering heat makes me want some cold milk, and the sticky tar burns my paws. Even the graceful and languid stretching of my gray and white body gives me no satisfaction.

I hear pots being moved, and I smell fried onions and meat I am getting excited. I can't keep still I stand up on my hind legs and continue trying to climb up the window even though I keep falling down. I tare at the panels with my clenched paws and extended nails I wiggle and squirm so hard. I scream wildly, not caring how ugly it makes me look. Finally I scratch on the glass window fiercely, for that usually gets results.

They're pretending they don't hear me even though I felt I was pushing right through the window. I'm worn out. I'll sit still and squint, my eyes and narrow my face in anger, collapse by body, straighten my whiskers, and sensuously wave my tail very, very low.

I hear someone opening 'the window'

End

"Sometimes Anybody Can Be Somebody"

BOOK TWO

Understand What Is Not Understood

Table Of Contents

February 2, 1995

Marcia Bennett - Bernier
New York City, N. Y

Dear Marcia,

I am so sorry to hear about your father I feel especially pained about it, and for you, because I have had these experiences and more.

Most of this is caused by, or aggravated by, the new definition of democracy that all people are equal, whether competent or not, conscientious or uncaring, good or evil. Many deaths can be attributed to this notion of equality.

I hope things are better for you Let me know, if I can be of help in any way.

Love,

When you get a chance, please send me the list, that you said you would, of all my additional items that you took – and the prices – so I can have a matching list – before we forget

August 3, 1995

Marcia Bennett - Bernier
New York City N Y

Dear Marcia,

Today is my birthday, and it is over 6 months since I wrote to you, and I haven't heard from you at all I hope nothing too troubling has kept you from doing so. As for me – I would have written sooner again but I have had, and still have a disturbing family problem that has been making me crazy, (I've been defrauded of all my assets by a relative, and I don't want to hurt the rest of the family)

I hope you have better news Please let me know what has been happening. I hope, especially, that you feel real well

Regards to Alex, I do wish we could have a real long talk Remember that you are always welcome where I am

Love,

March 24, 1996

Marcia Bennett - Bernier
New York City, N Y

Dear Marcia

I can't tell you how disappointed and hurt I was that you would not return my calls when I was in New York. I thought you would be pleased to return my unsold things

I am therefore forced to consider reporting the loss of my merchandise but to be sure I do not incorrectly report what you sold and owe me for, and the things you admit you still have, please send me this information now so I can check off from my lists I hope you are well and much happier.

Love,

April 5, 2000

Marcia Bennett - Bernier
New York City, N Y

Dear Marcia,

I keep waiting for you to keep your promises, and I am more disappointed than ever The things that you have admitted to having sold, you still haven't paid me for And you have not returned any of my most valuable items. For instance, whatever you returned I marked off and you only returned some of the paintings but none of the valuable ones. And that applies to everything, that you even bothered to return.

When I speak with someone on the phone, I usually take notes. So when you told me you stopped using my electric bed and folded it up to take up less space, I told you that you could sell it so I could get only $500. And you could keep the rest. And you agreed. This bed has a special motor which never needs repairs of any kind and this bed is not replaceable

Then when I had a customer for it for you, you suddenly told me that you don't know what happened to it. What would you think if I talked to you like that?

The same thing about the huge quartz – Maybe someone stole it. This quartz was so big and heavy that even the strongest man could not go off with it And it was a most unusual and beautiful specimen.

All the small and very desirable collectable items, you seem to have lost all records of and all memory of, so you ask me to send you the list and now you have remained silent since you saw the copies in your own handwriting What do you expect me to do? I have always, not only liked you very much, but trusted your honesty, and I was always concerned for your welfare

I wish you were capable of being more truthful with me. If you wish to pay me for the things you admit to have sold, then I will not include them in the police report

(P.s. Your boyfriend Alex accidentally admitted to me that he had the bed.)

My best wishes,

Marcia Bennett - Bernier

New York City N Y

Dear Marcia,

I still feel sorry for you - knowing that you will have to keep lying to yourself for the rest of your life -to cover your guilt -for stealing all my valued possessions (mine and my parents) knowing bow desperate I was to have to leave everything with you, who pretended to be a friend who could be trusted - all in the hope of saving my hopelessly dying husband.

Perhaps you can send me a copy of your dreams?

Marcia Bennett - Bernier
New York City, N. Y

Dear Marcia,

Your mouth kept going, going, going very fast like a guilty war machine Never stopping from spewing out your factory of lies

I used to defend you and I used to think you were capable of being a friend, and I couldn't help myself but feel sorrow for what I once thought of as a human being and as a friend

I always felt kindly toward you, and I couldn't help but feel sorry for you that you should need to prostitute yourself by perjuring yourself in order to steal everything from my family and me

In Memory of you,

Yes, my poor Marcia,   8-14-09

I still feel sorry for you – knowing that you will forever have
to keep lying to yourself for the rest of your days – to cover
your guilt – for stealing all my valued possessions (mine and
my parents) knowing how desperate I was to have to leave
everything with you, who pretended to be a friend who
could be trusted – all in the hope of saving my hopelessly
dying husband.

A solution for you would be for you to become a Catholic,
and then you can keep saying Hail Marys – all your days
and all your nights – to tell yourself what you want to
believe.

Dear Olga,

You are poisoning yourself with your thoughts. Instead of thinking of how you can solve each problem, you think how someone is at fault in not doing it for you

You keep reminding yourself constantly what and how someone else did it wrong, and especially how someone did it wrong only to you and against you.

This is the way you are poisoning yourself and it is the way to drive yourself mad, and that is the way mad becomes crazy.

You get mad when someone else doesn't know, or do, everything, but you don't think you are supposed to do or know everything. You forget that everyone is as human as you are.

You get mad when, something is not immediate for you, but no cure is immediate except death.

You get mad
You get mad
You get mad
You get mad

You can list all the things you are mad about, including me and everyone and everything, and then let us talk about it.

Love,

To The Town –

Our property that our parent's purchased unseen because they couldn't afford more had been owned by American Indians.

People came to get water on the property and called it "Long Leban Vaser".

There was (and is) their burial grounds which my Mother did not permit me to dig up. Which I wanted to do so much There is a cave up on the hill where there are Indian drawings and objects on the walls.

And now, the amount being used for those you do not pay taxes added on to the amount I was forced to pay with the threat of confiscation of my property and forced to remove all our life-long family buildings in order to protect a neighbor who kept breaking in to steal our stoves, refrigerators and antique furniture and belongings, to protect him in case he got hurt while doing this

Personal Letters

August 24, 1973

Mr Herbert Solon
New York City, New York

Dear Mr. Solon

I keep calling you endlessly and when I do reach you on the phone, you keep repeating that you are taking care of my case against Mr Sullivan, and you and another lawyer have been working on it, and you keep reminding me that you have paid $60 for serving papers on him and his nephew in October 1972 (to get him to return my money which you had advised and arranged for me to give him in the first place.) You took all my papers then (and you knew I had no copies) and all this time you have been reassuring me over and over that you completed the necessary steps, and that they were served and the SEC was notified and you assured me of success.

You repeatedly told me this on the telephone as well as the times you permitted me to come to your office. You said I would receive corroboration in the mail from you and your other lawyer. When I later reminded you that I had not, and that I still didn't know his name, and couldn't you give me his telephone no, so I could call him? I asked you for something in writing since I had been waiting for over a year. You became defensive and accused me of not trusting you. Then, for the first time, you actually said that neither of the men had been served because you didn't believe the nephew was legally responsible (although you were the one who had decided he was.) Until now you repeatedly told me that both were responsible and that he was actually served and that the SEC was holding him responsible for causing me to have had to hire another lawyer to get back my money from Mr. Dana to whom you had me pay $2,500 as a retainer fee. Mr. Dana also kept telling me for years that everything was being done but that it takes a great deal of time to get on the calendar, and other fantastic lies. It was only by accident that I learned that I was being deceived by him It was my dentist whose brother, also a lawyer, had overheard something about what was being done to me, and my dentist told me. (Of course to get my money back by another lawyer – although it was almost instantly – I had to pay an even higher fee.)

All these years I never suspected it was you who had my money all those years which you had Mr Dana pretend that he was the one, and of course my having paid it to him And all those years I never suspected it could be your fault and you kept making me believe it was the fault of Mr. Dana! It was only after your remark that I finally suspected and realized that the money returned to me through hiring a third lawyer, which had been possessed by you for years – and the matter completely and forever neglected – and yet you continued your endless lies over endless telephone calls! All this time this money was yours through Mr Dana, and that Mr. Dana was merely the person who took the money for you.

When I finally realized all the cruel harm you did and the years of hanging me in the air to toss slowly in the air, the thousands of telephone calls you requested from me and the numerous trips to your office – my hurt was so great that I could only respond impotently and therefore unable to do anything. I have been turning my other cheek for so long, and this, and you, are the last straw. You always claimed to be our friend and we trusted and believed you, and you betrayed our every trust and your every word

Even the money you took for filing a mortgage (You insisted on receiving it in cash but finally agreed to accept part of it by check) Always repeating that you were picking up the mortgage papers for me – and you would keep asking me to call you back endless times, and each time you begged me to wait because you were picking it up that day, the next, and whatever excuse you could make – or someone else was picking it up for you – or had picked it – and always telling me that it was definitely filed You would imply that I didn't trust you and you would get angry You even told me that you had picked it up and your papers were somewhere or other, and therefore I couldn't pick it up myself

And what about all the matters you supposedly did for my husband, and then you always kept what you were supposed to forward to him? I can't imagine what you did with the other people I recommended to you

And what about the most serious matter of all which involved my sister and her daughter, whose husband

Steven Bland was responsible for her being in a coma. You assured us that he and his wealthy family would pay the hospital bills, - and your concern and promises! Until all the witnesses disappeared (we were told the witnesses had been paid off) – and so much later when you returned some of my papers, and there, to our extreme surprise, I found the medical bills that had never even been submitted, but had been paid by my husband

It never occured to us that the man of the legal profession would be lying to his client again and again, and on such matters. In retrospect, I can't imagine how I could have been so deceived. I am still the innocent farm girl and stupidly trusting lamb who believed that all people have the integrity and morality that my very poor and completely uneducated farm parents instilled in me

The injuries and intellectual rape you have imprinted upon me are beyond imagination – and in a civilization run by your profession – is far greater than all the monetary losses you were responsible for on our behalf.

April 16, 1976

Mr. Oscar J. Cohen
New York City, New York

Dear Mr. Cohen –

I received your letter with Mr Solon's statement and did not answer sooner because I felt so outraged. As you yourself can easily see Since Mr. Solon lied to me about everything while I was his client, it is only natural that he would do no differently for himself.

I am enclosing a copy of the letter I wrote to him on August 1973 from which you can get a picture of some of the things that I know about and have proof. I am enclosing some of the details relating to the matters brought up

It took me a long time to realize that Mr. Solon is a phychopathic liar, for he appears so kindly and I really thought so well of him

September 30, 1977

Dear Mr Cohen

I will try to explain what happened on September 7th. I was assigned by Judge Schwartz to Judge Wolin. I waited in the room where Judge Wolin was to preside

I noticed that Mr Solon and Roth were busily coming and going repeatedly. After a while Mr. Roth (Mr Solon's attorney) came over to me and said I was to follow him to another room. I trustingly followed him and it was not until much later that I realized that I was led to a different judge, arranged by Mr. Roth. How else? The judge Mr Roth took me to was judge Sclar, who at first pretended as if he was helping me because he said to Mr Solon and Mr. Roth that I needed help because I was undefended. Very soon, I realized I was mistakenly naïve when none of my evidence was even looked at and instead Judge Sclar just looked down and said to Mr. Roth that all this is proof against myself.

I couldn't believe that it was possible for even the worst kind of human being to do and say such a thing and I immediately felt paralyzed by the hopelessness of it all. Then Mr. Roth, with a great act of Hollywood showmanship, said to me "Where did you get that manila envelope?" I didn't know what he was referring to and pointed to everything I had for him to show me He pointed to a folded piece of paper on which I had written some notes and dates about the Geico matter, and accused me of having stolen my papers from

Mr Solon's office! I expected the judge to inquire about this but he had no intention to do so I felt so hurt and by such a fantastical extreme trumped up lie, and realizing the judge was set up for this, that after hearing Mr. Solon's lies to questions asked him by the step-up-judge, so that when the judge asked me if I had any questions to ask Mr. Solon, I knew it was all useless, and all I could say was "You will all have to sleep with yourselves while remembering what you have done to me.: Judge Sclar dismissed the case. I spoke to Mr. Friel, assistant district attorney who advised me to inform you, the bar association and to go to Criminal Court about Mr. Solon's remark about having a bullet put through my head and about Mr Roth accusing me of stealing my papers

My problem is that I am afraid that Mr Solon who claimed to be friendly with some Mafia clients will carry out his threat

September 1, 1993

Mazel Davis
East NY Savings
New York, NY

Dear Mr Davis

American Savings Bank of Florida has informed me that you have not received my savings book which Gary, manager, has mailed to you because the US post office refuses to deliver your mail when addressed to
East NY Savings Bank
Peter Cooper Branch
East 20 St, and 1st Ave
N Y, N Y. 10021?

And that you request a ten dollar fine from me instead of fining the post office for keeping the mail, instead of, at least, returning it to the sender

Now since I don't want another book, and don't need another book for transferring my account, I would like to have an explanation from you that has a iota of rationality to it

I realize the educators today do not believe in logic, and that logic may not return for at least one or two generations from now, but even if you want to make everything relevant to nothing, I absolutely can not pay for something I don't want and don't need

So perhaps you can mail some forms for me to sign so that I can withdraw at least part of my money until you bravely contact your post office

I am enclosing a copy of my receipt from the Am. Savings Bank sent to you about two months ago with my book, etc. – which has my account and amount of balance (before interest and direct deposits)

June 14, 1960

Committee on Requirements
New School for Social Research

Gentlemen:

I wish to thank you for refusing me re-admission to your school. You have thus spared me from further years of fruitless and non-educational "education" in your school.

It was the persistent suggestions of someone in your school that I re-applied for admission. This was in opposition to all my feelings because of the irrationality which I and many others have experienced from your previous faculty and past heads of the school. And at this person's insistence and reassurance of the improvement of your school heads and faculty, I again asked for admission

Now even you consider the previous administration as adequate judges in grading me poorly, and yet, at the same time, you consider them inadequate in admitting me as a PhD student

This in itself shows me that the irrationality of the school is continuing in the new administration, and such a school can not deserve my respect Thank you for not accepting me

Sincerely yours,

Dear Jean,

I addressed the envelope to you a long time ago but I am finally writing to you today. Partly because I get so involved in doing nothing that I forget about the passing of time But mostly it is that I am so stressed trying to do things, and avoiding doing them, and being frustrated because of it.

And it is very hard for me to talk to someone when there is no response - E-mail helps that to some extent because it is so fast I had a copy of the New York Post yesterday and it has so much more of what I know and am interested in than the local papers - but I hate to pay so much for it down here. I miss so much of the news by not seeing it In some ways, it is like living in a different country Perhaps you can fill me in on with some of it. Looking forward to hearing from you

PS
I am enclosing the article about Hillary that I told you about

Dear Jenny,

I'm not sure I know what you want to know It would be mainly lab work and usually you get information in different instructors and find out different areas of study that particularly interest you and which is available to you. You have to start somewhere, do you want to be there before you begin?

Your father said you are dissatisfied with the school and that you are lonely Everyone is lonely when they start somewhere new What do you expect? The school sounded so wonderful to me I don't know what the instructors are like, but there must be some that are good.

Do you feel you are not appreciated enough? It is not their purpose to replace parents and friends. If you spend your time really studying hard, you will not be lonely much longer. I promise you that. Let me know what you think your problems are.

Love, Your aunt

Dear Sadye,

Since I have no idea of who or what was said to whom, I feel it is necessary for me to disappear so as not to upset you so. Your resentment toward me goes way back from the beginning of time, and I do not know how to alleviate it

I do feel saddened by this, but I just have too much to bear without adding this, whatever it is. I have really tried hard to help all the ways I know how. Even Shirley-the-Great said to me reproachfully "Why don't you let Philip buy the place? Does Shirley really believe that I have been stopping him? Is that what you believe?

When I told her that Philip has been saying this for months but so far he hasn't. I said to her "I'm not sure how reliable he is because he is disturbed. Shirley answered me angrily "I don't find him disturbed at all". I said: "All right, if he is not disturbed, then it is I who am disturbed. It is what she believes and it is apparently what you believe. And so it is and what else can I say?

Dear Sondra,

Misunderstandings occur very easily. I am un-aware of what terrible things I must have said, or if someone else misstated it for me. I apologize for whatever I said or didn't say. I do sometimes make satiric remarks, which not everyone understands unless they know me well

How many Hail Mary's would get your forgiveness? Or what atonement is acceptable?

Understand What Is
Not Understood

PART ONE & PART TWO

The Memoirs And Essays

Formal Letters

The letters that follow, both formal and personal are important to the Author to include in this book They express her feelings during certain periods and events in her life.

You will understand after you have read the letters

This is my first writing of a page on the Internet

There is nothing I would like to say that should be put on the screen for people to not understand I will add more in the future – some things like what I am and am not saying.

New York Post
Editorial Department

July 31, 1990

Answer to
Sheik Wagdi Ghonieon
and his Brooklyn College followers

I was not aware that I am a descendant of the apes until you informed me And I am most grateful to you for this information because until now I never understood why you hate me so. At last I understand!

I like apes even though I didn't know that I was related to them. I really like them better than some people.

Sincerely,

August 10, 1991

Mr Thomas Sobol
Education Commissioner
NY

Dear Mr. Sobol

I understand you are heading a project which I am totally interested in, and I would like to offer my help, salary free.

I am particularly interested in the minority problem, as I have been studying this for twenty years. I would like to know how many minority types are to be studied and which minorities are going to be included and which are going to be excluded.

I am a clinical psychologist (not a historian) and I am offering my help free, under your guidance.

Sincerely yours,

Daily News
New York

Dear Mr. Crouch,

Ref: your August 3, 1997 Article

It is interesting that you mention one single country that is receiving money from U.S. You forgot to mention how much Arafat gets, how much Egypt gets, and the others.

If our politicians weren't giving so much to the others, then Israel would not need to accept anything to defend itself and Democracy

Sincerely, A Devoted Reader

Woody Allen
New York City

Dear Woody,

I love your loudly - heard evaluation of Israel!

I think you are so right, and I hope you will prove it to the world by going there yourself and standing right between the innocent Palestinians and the wicked Israelis, to demonstrate your even-handedness.

In this way you can instantly become the New-World Messiah, and save the world.

Sincerely yours,

Mr. Dershowitz
Warner Book, Harvard Law School

Dear Mr. Dershowitz,

I am particularly interested in the concept of justice, and therefore found your book "Just Revenge" as most important

I was, however, disappointed in its ending Your ending would be very pleasing to readers in general, but it is not based on reality. There is just too much evidence that genetic inheritance is not meaningless. There can be exceptions where the line of inheritance is stronger or weaker from one source, but it is not eradicated that easily

I do wonder how you would have ended it if you had not dismissed that fact?

Sincerely yours,

August 23, 2007

County Division of Planning
Government Center
NY 12701-9908

Dear Sirs

I have not answered you any sooner because of my pained feelings regarding what was our lifetime homes.

I was forced, by those who give themselves the power, by threats, to remove our buildings. This was in order to protect the neighbor below us and others from injuring themselves when they would break into and steal our possessions.

I find it hard to understand why the punishment is for the victim instead of the victimizer. Perhaps you could explain this to me

Sincerely yours,

September 10, 2007

Kathy Sprague, Town Assessor
New York

Dear Town Assessor.

Instead of protecting us, we were forced by threats to remove our lifetime home buildings in order to protect our neighbor below us from hurting himself when he kept breaking in our buildings to steal our belongings

Now that taxes still keep increasing, even under such circumstances, can you please tell us how much I am paying extra for the people who call themselves a new "religion" in order not to pay their taxes?

And why have these neighbors been allowed to have their electric poles on our property without our permission?

Sincerely yours,

January 7, 2009

Laurie Dutcher
Tax Collector
NY 14240

Dear Ms. Dutcher

I am enclosing one check for the three separate bills for school taxes

You have been very kind in responding to me before, and I would so appreciate if you would provide me with some additional information, such as the amount or percentage of my taxes that I am paying for those who do not pay taxes. Perhaps I can feel good knowing the amount of charity I am providing for others

You are most unusual in answering me before and I truly appreciate and honor you for this

Sincerely yours,

Miami Herald
Executive Editor

Dear Mr Clifton,

Ref. "The Neighbors" April 1999 "Families Of severely disabled face dilemma over what to give up" by Mireidy Fernandez

The D'Angelos's 25-year old son who is severely disabled, has a day companion and receives 96 diapers each month, but uses six diapers a day To toilet train him, they had a therapist for six months, and the family had to give that up in favor of more diapers

I would like to recommend a solution for you to give to his constitutionally creative lawyer: Why not have the toilet training therapist spend even a small part of those six months and teach the loving parents, as well as the companion, how to toilet train the son, and even teach the Aunt and Grandparents who all love him?

P S. Enclosing copies of your article with pictures.

Sincerely,

Lighthouse for the Blind

Dear Mr. Metcalf

You will never be forgotten by so many of us

In this way, you have already attained immortality!

All our love and best wishes.

April 3, 2003

Mr. Alan Nichols, President
Lighthouse for the Blind
Miami, FL

Dear Mr. Nicholas.

As a current and long-time member of the Lighthouse for the Blind, I feel the need to involve you as their volunteer President of the Board in a situation that involves an ex-employee, Mr Larry Lawhorn

It seems that I am the so-called chosen person who does not worry about stating an opinion that is shared by many, and thus, I am taking this opportunity to do just that.

I have the good fortune, or perhaps the misfortune, of being privy to hearing whispered comments from many of the participants expressing their sadness about the loss of Larry Lawhorn and the way he was dismissed

You need to know that people are not happy. The joy we have experienced during our time there with the previous administration, made the Lighthouse a very special place for the clients to feel wanted and cared for

Larry was responsible for those feelings. He is an integral part of creating an atmosphere conducive to the needs of the clients and sometimes beyond their needs. It has turned into a pervasively saddened environment without him there to lend a helping hand and good work. A certain somberness has replaced the contented climate that existed prior to his departure.

We are all feeling devastated and an emptiness for losing Larry. We admired him tremendously for his accomplishments for the Lighthouse He worked seven days a week and long hours He did the networking for the entire Lighthouse and on his own time. He volunteered numerous extra hours and even paid for many extras to save the Lighthouse many thousands of dollars

The staff, clients, and volunteers are all distraught by such a great loss. It is not easy to maintain a devoted and committed employee, and we feel that the new Director should have more carefully made her decision and perhaps asked the long-time clients for input before making such a destructive decision.

On behalf of many of us, please consider bringing Larry Lawhorn back to his previous position at the Lighthouse, where he is much needed and sadly missed.

Sincerely yours,

New York Post
Joyce Brothers

Dear Dr. Brothers,

In your column of May 11th in the 'New York Post' referring to the book "Confronting Crime" by Elliot Currie, with which you say you agree, you say inequality of wealth leads to crime.

I would appreciate it if you would clarify this by answering these questions:

1. When in our history did we have greater equality?
2. Do you feel that you yourself commit no crimes only because you are not in want?
3. Why is it that so many people who are in want do not commit any crimes?

I would appreciate your comments. I am enclosing a self addressed stamped envelope for a personal reply.

Sincerely yours,

President George W. Bush

The White House

Dear President Bush,

I have no reason to defend anyone except for the obvious purpose of justice or fairness. And since you appear to be really working for justice, which is rare in people of great power, I would like to bring to your attention for examination and correction, without prejudice, which appears to be a lack of justice in relation to the treatment of Pollard vs Robert Hanssen.

I am referring to a documentary shown February 18, 2002 on T V channel A&E about Robert Hanssen, the worst American spy, who was responsible, not only for twenty years of treason, murder of American FBI agents, and other untold harm, He is given even the rights to keep his pension, his home, etc, and is treated with compassion and respect for being a religious man.

In the case of Pollard, he not only never even gave information to an enemy country, but gave information to Israel that had not only been promised to them, but was a promise not being kept, even when it was a serious danger to them from Iraq.

I realize that it is part of human nature, for most people to seek scapegoats in order to make themselves feel and look better But this never really helps them at all and only creates more injustices in the future, for themselves, as well as for others

I do not know if you, or anyone else will even read this, but I hope I am mistaken about that, and that somehow I might be informed that you at least heard me. This matter seems to have some similarities to the Dreyfus Affair.

P.S.
I am enclosing corroborating data

Respectfully yours,

President Bill Clinton

The White House

Dear President Clinton,

You told us that you do not know what "is" is Personally I find what "is" just is. No matter how I define it

For instance, when death occurs, whether I define it as going to heaven, or being reincarnated, or any of the other definitions - no matter what I call it, or describe it as -I find that it always means that it is And I have to accept what is, no matter how I try to fool myself. I find it difficult to even fool others, though I say: "He is still here with me"

I do wish you would tell me how I too could make what is to not be, the way you can

Sincerely,

Note – I received an answer from President Bill Clinton. His answer to me was "he was not going to answer my letter"

August 25, 1999

Dear Sally,

At last I see why lawyers are unable to help me with a justice trust! It is because lawyers are taught not to understand what justice means.

For example, lawyer President Clinton, a Rhodes and Oxford scholar, admitted he doesn't even know what "is" is. He suffered such pain from this lack of knowledge that he admitted it before the entire world.

Mr. Jacobowitz sent you the information for which he had charged me $648 80. The information still secret from me; only the charges were not secret. A lawyer's way of thinking? And now you feel it only right that I be expected to pay again for the same information now given to you?

You helped lawyer Saul Feder steal $2,500 from me by generously feeding him unbelievable misinformation which his criminal mind found very useful. Of course, it was not intentional on your part, but does a lawyer's justice mean that I should pay for others' mistakes as well as my own? Is this the meaning of justice?

Sincerely, with love,

National Tax Payers Union

Alexandra, VA
5-24-07

Dear Hopefuls,

Please tell me how you imagine you can possibly accomplish getting the fair tax passed-'-considering the massive I.R.S. Federal employees who profit from this unfair mess and would not give it up, nor the endless accountants and lawyers and all their relatives, friends, and their attachments? If you could do this, I would certainly love to help in every way.

Sincerely yours,

And the same like my sister who once brought me a valuable gift of a pretty pair of panties I didn't wear them because they were too pretty to wear When I finally decided to do so, they were too small for me and I was unable to get them on at all I had no one I could talk to about this and I couldn't confess this to my sister who had been so generous to me

I never made myself comfortable in my own home, just as I couldn't feel comfortable or belonging in my mother's home - all my life I didn't feel free to make myself comfortable in my own bed, in my own kitchen, I had to clutter or mess everything up, to feel as always that there was no place for me. Also I treated my home as if it was not my home later on in life

I bought many things I admired and then I had no one to give them to I wanted many things but I also didn't want anything Or maybe I stopped wanting anything I didn't know what to do with them if I had them. When I thought I wanted something, it was never the right thing anyhow I was most pleased when I stopped myself from buying something because everything created added problems for me

The 85 Dollars Hourly Fee

I once contracted someone to help me put order into some of my manuscripts I had to sign an agreement In this contract it stated that the payment was eighty-five Dollars an hour This made me feel anxious and hurried I was not young enough to think so fast and I asked for a complete estimated price of each work instead. But this person felt very good at yelling me that it would be only eighty-five dollars an hour Instead it made me feel very sad Some of my past memories flashed through my mind Eight-five Dollars was money for a whole year's food for a family of six

For Sabbath, Friday night and Saturday dinner at noon, my family would have chicken That is how I learned to love the chicken bones, rather than the meat, and that is the only part I like and enjoy today

Eight-five Dollars, my unconscious said it was a sin on my part But I didn't go to beauty parlors like women would go weekly and religiously, as if it were life itself, to have someone else paint their nails and even their toes I didn't spend money on all sorts of things that women usually feel they are supposed to

Yet, when to my surprise, I found out I have money, it was like something foreign to me I felt it didn't belong to me though I alone earned it and I never allowed myself to be dependent and supported by anyone

Uncovering my subconscious mentality was not an easy thing to do, neither for me nor for most of us So what was I supposed to do about this and how did I feel? I couldn't expect this person to understand, although she was well intentioned and wanted to learn to understand me for her own sake Was it another charity for me to give to? This woman thought she deserved these eighty-five dollars an hour but it made me feel guilty to even think of it It made me feel so very guilty to my parents, and to my siblings I wasn't able to do it for them

In fact, I felt guilty for everyone that it was my inner self Of course I would never know what terrible past histories make up my past inheritance, but I carried them on forever The unending pain I kept experiencing was much more than the money part, it was a never-ending abandonment as of death, an actual killing of me

Health

I spent my money on various therapists The therapists never listened to what I was saying or trying to say, they were into their own notions of what they believed, wanted, or expected

MENTAL HEALTH

As soon as I had completed high school, I left for the city to find work and to find psychological help I was introduced to three therapists

One young psychiatrist said what I needed was sex and he would take care of that if I agreed He wanted to introduce me to a mental institution and to have sex with him as a cure So for me that was the end of him

The second one said what I needed was help getting a place to live better, help with a job, etc While I needed more than that, I did need that first of all He was a much older psychoanalyst and I felt hopeful Perhaps he would have been the best choice, or at least the less harmful.

But the third one was who held my interest He was an older experienced psychoanalyst who had been analyzed by Freud This is what I wanted and I chose this doctor But instead of his helping me with treatment he decided to marry me and that was the end of my therapy I didn't quite feel right about him but how could I refuse Freud, and so I felt rewarded and let it happen. What followed was his advise and everything about him was wrong for me It took endless years for me to learn that his unconscious needs would be harmful for me I did not understand this of course Not until very much later after it was over and too late to be useful or understood Just failure every way and for both of us, understanding never existed, only pain

Throughout my life I went to many therapists for help Some of them were famous and they had their famous theories But none were able to hear me, to listen to me,

219

to find me They all had their theories that I had to fit into, and were very annoyed that I didn't fit into their preconceived notions, and blamed me for that

There were a few who even wanted me to work with them, to train me There was even one who was interested enough to charge me so little that I couldn't refuse his offer of treatment, though I was particularly not pleased to accept him as a therapist In the end my mistrust proved correct But at first little things and his desire to try to work with me won my trust Until he did what was a duplication of what must have created the problem

This is what I've had been saying to psychiatrists for years It was not only a waste of time, money and energy but a waiting for life to begin, to be creative, to function, and be constructive Then there was the wasting and decay of my fertility, I was still going to psychiatrists, and still no one heard me (I had the wrong Doctor!) Calling me names, that I used people, that I was spiteful, a manipulator and a schemer It was only like throwing stones at a dead person I couldn't hear it It neither hurt nor helped because I was elsewhere where no one reached me I was desolate and alone I had waited for Godot, until it was too late

My ambivalence and this crave for bodily contact, pregenital, stemmed from that I could not accept mother So I paid someone to listen to me but they really didn't. They were preoccupied with their own thoughts regarding me and therefore didn't get to even try to understand me. There were those therapists who did not see me as being so normal. But those people were the ones who were perhaps even less so than myself, most of them were projecting their abnormalities on to me and not at all seeing it in themselves

I could hardly understand how I was able to go through so many years of my life and doing so many things and being seen by most people as a normal person, and yet not being there, not being whole I was carrying so much emotional pain, something like the Ancient Mariner, and often I was too conscious of my impending end At the same time being many things to many people I saw most of mankind that way to some extent, with times of re-activated pain I would go back and forth in my thinking and it was repeated in my analyses and with my first husband, the analyst, as with my mother It was nothing but a repeat of my mother and me

I neither understood myself nor what my problems were about I did not understand what I covered up and so all the therapists did not understand me Whatever I could make out and understand I would get from books Books, were my friends, people were not

I always waited for each analyst to kick me out and be through with me, abandoning me

Dr Wilhelm Reich

With all that, and more, it was Dr. Wilhelm Reich who marveled at that he called me almost "normal" He said he thought it was because I was not brought up in a city At that time Wilhelm Reich was not accepting patients anymore who were not therapists and therefore referred me to a number of possible choices that were taught by him But most of them didn't want to take the chance to treat me because I had been married to a known therapist

The Christian Psychiatrist

There was one therapist with strong Christian beliefs who seemed to want to work with me even though or maybe because I was Jewish I wanted to be able to trust him until I had proof I could not I felt he was the type of a person who could not like me mostly because of my religion In a sense it ended up that way

Because he planned on going on vacation for the summer he wanted me to make an extra trip I felt it was not worth it for me to make such a long extra trip so soon, so I offered to pay for the time anyway, but he understood it as tricking him because I was a Jew, and he said he did not want to see me again

It was complicated to go to see him One day it was bad weather but he insisted I come in anyhow Once I arrived he refused to take me because I was late and I got very emotional and expressed my discontent He could not handle my reaction and didn't want me to act that way in his office because other people might hear it

I felt rejected What was the point in having therapy in which I could not express myself? He planned to go on vacation for the summer, so he wanted me to make an extra trip before he left, which I felt may not be worth doing, for a session because he was so far from me He felt he could not trust me to be there because he felt I was tricky because I was a Jew But I told him I would pay him He decided not to see me anymore

Dr Willie

In the case of Dr Willie, I did not realize the way he felt because he seemed so sure of himself when he was in his mood swing and because of his background, which did not include poverty and because of his education I could not realize how he felt because he never spoke about it, never confided in anyone

Dr Gold

Dr Gold didn't allow me to talk but told me what was no good about me When I felt bad, I sounded bad and he would get angry I thought that some people become hypochondriacs because they are not permitted to say, "I feel terrible I feel unhappy, I feel upset" Instead they say "I have a headache, or a stomachache, or a cold"

When anyone expressed anger towards me, I withdrew, I simply disappeared from everything, which was very bad I did feel miserable and there was no one else at the time I could talk to I guessed one had to pay someone to be allowed to talk, and even then, maybe not what you felt the need to talk about

The Black Therapist

Even poor Jesus was killed only once - or so I've been told
But I've been killed many times

When I was so ill and told I was dying by my doctors
and I was having emotional trouble about my first husband,
I thought maybe it was mental Maybe I was crazy and, and,
if I was crazy I wouldn't know it, and therefore had to try
to get help I knew this black co-worker who was considered
the best therapist of the clinic We both worked at Doctor
Wertham's free clinic in Harlem I saw him twice and he
said he didn't know that white people could have problems
I felt he couldn't help me because he believed that a white
person could not feel so much pain, fear, and suffering

When I heard that I thought there was no point in
seeing him again How would he be able to help me with
this kind of attitude? I couldn't believe that anybody could
think that way, that white people are not human For him
only black people were humans and had problems

Dr Tierstein And His Female Assistant

The fear of being examined by this other doctor was big
She asked me if I thought she would hurt me. I told her she
made me feel guilty by being angry with me. The terror
that pervaded my life, the tightening up in my eyes and
head and shoulders and arms, like an infant afraid of being
dropped into the water and all the energy leaving the lower
part of the body That woman therapist who believed that
all children were taught to be afraid being boxed in alive

Then I started feeling bad again I had felt quite cheerful and well days before and I wondered at the change Now I was back to feeling strained, blurred sight, dizziness, pain in the eyes, and as if I were feverish, and as if I were being eaten up by viruses, and losing my hair and tightening around my ears

After 20 Years Of Therapy

By then it was over 20 years that I had gone to how many therapists? I didn't know that I was more miserable by then because I knew more, because I had less belief, or because I was much older, and my life had been related to waiting for help I hadn't been able to help myself either I probably circumvented it whenever I came close to what I needed

I couldn't be loving to anybody or felt myself loved unless I was fed food and fed knowledge and fed conversation I started killing myself off with the amount of bad food I kept eating I tried everything I thought would comfort me When one food did not work I kept trying another and another - but nothing, nothing appeased me The nearest thing that momentarily worked was the smell and taste of eggs Perhaps I had to keep proving to myself that I could feed myself, and didn't need anyone else for survival

Self-Therapy

Because of my fear of escalators, it was so very important for me to use escalators because in some buildings there was no other way, I worked very hard in my dreams and in every way I tried to reach my unconscious I wanted to find the reason for my extreme fear I finally brought back a memory I was climbing a ladder to the attic when I was a small child, age three perhaps. I felt so relieved and thought that was so simple that I would remember it always, and my fear was magically gone I was able to use the escalator! But soon some part of the memory was either not complete or was lost, and my fear returned – even stronger

Self-Reflections

From being praised in school of having a beautiful handwriting to scribbling handwriting as a defense or not wanting others to be able to read and know what I was saying or thinking If I were to go on what I really wanted - always my inadequacies struck me first, like a blocked door - and I couldn't get further. I didn't know where to go to begin Nevertheless I realized I couldn't look to others for help that was within me Not with my wandering sickness caused by being a Jewess How could one make up time? If that couldn't be done, there was no hope

One of the friendly instructors at a place where I took computer lessons made an appointment for me with a neurologist/psychiatrist and told me I had to go and see him After examining and questioning me, he said "You need to choose more intelligent friends"

I met people who were very nice to me that morning yet I felt a terrible need to cry When I got home I took a hot bath immediately to keep myself from eating again, from swallowing everything I had the radio on in order not to feel alone, though not listening to the music But I felt it in my throat, the need to sing very loudly It was like being starved for food I so much had to sing, and after that I didn't need to cry There were sensations in the lower part of the left chest, and I was able to breathe better

It is too bad I was not a recognized singer then I wouldn't have had to feel so miserable all the time I was offered an opportunity in that direction and ran away even from that, because I had been fore-warned by the leader that being a soloist would attract jealousy from the rest of the chorus

The Fearful Daughter

As a daughter I was terrified of criticism, and of confrontation and being caught in a mistake frozen as if my life stopped To be berated was the emotional equivalent of execution But in most cases I was terrified of my unpleasant emotions, especially anger All negative emotions seemed to have equal weight and were equally crushing So reactive and so sensitive that I cocooned myself into anonymity to avoid attracting attention, I subordinated and protected myself either by a controlling person or isolating myself

I read in one of my reference books "Many adults and teachers misread introverts and deep thinkers and label them shy children, even thinking them to be stupid Shyness is a reaction to being denigrated or being a role model

A loving father that is proud of his daughter never

shuts her up and only couches for her greatness This daughter is raised with the idea that she can do anything, like becoming president etc On the other side this kind of daughter has often a mother that is dependent on her daughter A daughter, whose father is achievement oriented If a daughter that is cherished by both parents and doesn't feel rejected she usually is turning into what is called a female achiever

And a competitive daughter treated like a protégés who is nurtured by her mother and father as a role model She is usually adored by both parents and has permission from them to compete and disagree with assertiveness She receives paternal acceptance and affection "I had neither acceptance nor affection or any of these My parents would have loved to be such parents but couldn't just like I couldn't

Because of an absent father, I picked men who treated me badly or were emotionally unavailable "You can't get hurt if you're rejected by losers" I had a fear of dependence But there was also a fear of independence and not being sure I belong anywhere As a fearful daughter I had a critical mother I could not do anything without my mother's approval So the rage was turned inwards There existed a symbiotic attachment to my mother and a fear of my father, not being able to defend myself

When I realized I needed to give up trying to please people I felt that my own needs were wrong, I felt that I would never be able to get needs met

*　*　*

Later in life I was trying to get to my unconscious to help find myself I was aware of nerves moving about to my right It made me feel ugly, or reminded me of being so I was aware of wanting to change the look in my eyes I was aware of my habit of staring blankly in avoidance, of the pressure of my teeth against each other that felt so big I was aware of trying to be aware I was aware of holding immobile my legs, my knees down, of my adolescence fantasy of being crippled in the legs and then not having to do anything I was aware of my identification with my mother and dishonesty in hiding under a little girl innocence

I was aware that I felt better when people weren't so nice, and then I could be meaner and less inhibited I was aware of my meanness and inhibitions I remember my father's anger, which made me feel fearful and unsafe I had deep imprints, repressed memories, until age 10 The illnesses I suffered were results of bits of frozen history In some way I had blinded myself not to see things that were too unpleasant, and I believed I had shut off my hearing not to hear so much criticism That might have also been how my vision and hearing were diminished

PHYSICAL HEALTH

As a child, I felt I was allowed to be sick when I had high enough fever But I was never allowed to feel upset or bad about things I had to be extremely sick to be allowed to be sick I would go to school with temperature But I also wanted to go for I'd feel guilty when I wasn't very sick

When I finished high school I was expected to go to the City in New York and get a job I went to the girl's Y and the cheapest room was for three residents I felt happy to be with two other rural girls and we decided to walk around the area and get familiar with the surroundings As we passed a drug store, one of the girls said she would like to stop and have a drink She ordered a citrus of magnesia and so we did the same

When we returned to the Y we cheerfully greeted the woman in charge by mentioning that we had a bellyache Her duty was to care for the residents and she kindly felt we should have a doctor see us The doctor examined us and said we have appendicitis

The woman in charge arranged for us to go to the best midtown eastside hospital, and everything would be free It sounded like so much fun to be together with my two new wonderful friends, the best doctors, the best hospital, food and lots of ice cream

In the end, with great regret and disappointment, I decided not to go I said to myself that I've had many bellyaches, but I didn't have my appendix removed each time

Very sadly I then waited for their happy return, which

didn't turn out to be so happy One girl lay down on her bed, turned to the wall and wept The other girl said there was nothing wrong with their appendix And then the woman in charge of our care told me, - very apologetically - that I had to leave the Y because I had not abided by its rules I had to leave the Y, and I never saw the girls again I was alone once more

Much later, I entered a tiny elevator and stood against the back wall A large number of young people, out for lunch, pushed into it It seemed dangerously packed full and I was unable to move out Having recently had a similar experience, which caused that elevator to fall, I expressed my concern about it

"Sickie" said one of these young very sturdy girls "Sickie, sickie, sickie", she kept repeating all the way down As we finally walked out together in the same direction down the street, I said "I'm glad I'm making you feel so good When you're older, you will be able to understand" She answered "You're the sickie lady, you're the one who is morbid"

I thought what a pity that that I had the experience of the fall when it was she who could have learned from it

Laughing Gas

In my life I've wept only a very few times One time it was when I was given "laughing" gas to surgically remove my wisdom teeth I needed to weep so badly to respond to my unconscious associations, but I painfully stopped myself because of the embarrassment for the people there I was afraid of the resentment by the dentist and that he would bawl me out in verbal punishment, as I was accustomed

Homeopathy

I would look at myself in the mirror to try to help me cry This was what I needed more than anything else in the world To find my own cry to- for- myself, and then I could forgo all husbands and all people, and all things I wanted my cry back, my right and ability to cry again I went to a homeopathic physician and told him that I needed something to help make me able to cry He did give me something and somehow I was able to cry just a little

Ears

I was very ill from massive antibiotics for ear infection and these almost constant pains in my neck I feared, if not already so, it would develop and break down into cancer, perhaps of the lymph system or throat

I didn't only feel it on the inside of my mouth but also way down in my throat I kept pouring in hot drinks but the congestion would not leave me, and I got no relief at all Perhaps that's where the cry was It's like a fire that could not be put out But if it was crying that was checked why should it cause heat and congestion? If this inflammation kept going down further and further, it would leave the parts above and give me relief there or would it torture the whole

And the nurse - after I questioned her so much about the x-rays and my concern about the rays - she went on for a while how safe it was - and then began to show her fear for herself - having been convinced by my fear instead of convincing me about its safety

Doctor Breslov examined my eats and said "Your hearing problem began when you were very young, maybe born with it" He was the first one to recognize this about my hearing, but of course it had gotten worse I asked him if he was Russian He said "I am from Russia but I am not Russian I am a Jew and in Russia it is a crime to be a Jew"

I was so sick as the result of an ear infection and I was told I must take antibiotics because otherwise the infection would affect my brain So my first husband gave me massive doses of antibiotics Which was Chloromycetin, I was getting worse and doctors said I had to continue or I would die – later I was told I was dying I never told them about my husband giving me antibiotics in such large doses He was actually murdering me I didn't know whether he knew this or didn't know it. The doctor then told me I had to try exploratory surgery An appointment was made The only thing that saved me from that was my realistic fear that I could not survive anesthesia because I was unable to breathe and I therefore cancelled the hospital arrangement This enraged the doctors It was only one of my almost killings

I kept going to doctors hoping for a different diagnosis My illness made my body so dead and my emotions were connected to all sorts of negative feelings I finally thought maybe I was crazy and didn't know it So I went to endless attempts of therapies, whatever I seemed to find Of course nothing helped when I was so physically sick I had to pay a nurse to sit in like a child all night not to be alone because I could hardly breathe and of course could not lie down.

Riding in a bus to see the doctors – no seat – color sky blue and had to look at blue colors – boy and energy into my knee Filled with phlegm The doctors wanted to open me up to see if they could find the cause – at the last moment I cancelled and caused resentment but I felt since I could not breathe, I would be worse off under anesthesia and I would surely die, but the doctors did not think that way

It seemed to be a help to sleep at night in the living room and work during the day in the bedroom I didn't know why I decided to move back into the bedroom near the telephone because I feared to get a stroke

Throat And Chest

One time I was on the train to Florida with a sore throat They could drop me off wherever they wanted and so I drank three large cups of coffee and I threw up and felt better afterwards I was allowed to continue on the train

I noticed lines on my legs just leaning at something There were marks from even loose clothing, no elasticity for hours I felt this pain under my arms and neck There was mucus under my chin Could mucus be in my head?

I was feeling better after almost two hours of relaxing on my buttocks, and having cried and exercised But I woke up in middle of the night with terrible contractions in the throat, shoulders, arms and head, eyes, shutting out something as though it was a matter of life and death, and now I was terribly sick again as if it was the Oedipus feelings and thoughts

Eyesight

At night toward late afternoon, I couldn't think or do things By then I was worn out by conflicts and because I couldn't see well I couldn't see well during the day either but better of course than at night How was the best way for me to spend the dark hours?

When that very nice lady in the eye doctors office called me and told me I was near normal in my left eye and that I could drive, I was ecstatic with happiness How could this miracle have occurred, since I never had normal vision before? But if I was normal why couldn't I tell when the light was red or green? Why couldn't I see it at all even when I put on dark glasses? Why couldn't I tell when it is a bus or a huge truck until it was right there upon me? Why did I lack the depth perception in being able to see when the sidewalk was not even, and I crashed and was badly injured? Why would no person whom I knew let me drive? Why did I suffer when I had to sit in a front seat while someone drives because it looked to me that we were too close to everything and we were about to hit another car?

And when handwriting, and I thought I was writing on the next line, I often found I had written on top of the writings on the above line Please tell me what was it that was wrong

Vision, Hearing And Memory

The therapists who worked in the rehabilitation center kept asking me whether I felt pain every time I was doing their exercises I didn't know how to really answer them because I was so used to discomforts of some kind, that I was not aware of what was happening when it did It seemed so natural to me that even when I was now losing more of my vision, hearing, memory, and everything that was happening to me, that it was as if it had already happened to me before it actually did Perhaps this was proof of our re-living our lives after 'death It seemed to me more like a preparation for dying, because this is what we must do.

Actually there was a time when I tried so very hard to teach my past subconscious and my feelings of abandonment, with the surprising result that I actually found myself in the desert, my body deeply covered in sand, trying to save myself from choking to death, left there to die

A loss of a job, a partner, or marriage or physical illness combined with imprinted material such as early loss of a parent, etc can cause neurosis and psychosis

ANXIETY AND "DECAY"

I passed by the picture of myself, which I had hidden away in the closet I had meant to get rid of it because the painter had specifically been told not to erase the character lines but had ignored me and made it look "nice" But now since I was marked with too many lines, I looked at the picture differently and decided to bring it out in the open, as an expression and acceptance of having once been young

When I had been very young, I would do whatever I could to conceal my looks, because I felt threatened by it Then later, when grown, I was always criticized for looking the way I did. People didn't know how and why I tried to make myself not noticed, invisible – my hair worse than plain, no makeup, and the plainest of clothes

More and more, had I been observing my physical degradation? I could see the lines in my neck and on my hands There was less healing of scars I witnessed the breakdown of tissues on my legs My first noticeable decay was the beginning of graying in my hair when my marriage broke up With all the tears inside, I was dehydrating My skin was shriveling on my neck, face, and hands Misery was engraved into my face and head and no way to erase it, like a stamp of death if not removed I worked to get it out on the surface, and then it was replacing all else Something was wrong with all the therapies

The problem was when you get older, other people see it too (besides yourself- having become fixed expression) and then mostly they see that and nothing else That is why many people don't like older people because their pains and miseries show more than anything else The fresh full flesh and easier smiles are less visible I didn't even know what my face looked like I looked different to different people, but to myself I saw only my expression printed onto my face This expression of weeping held in and stopped, the only part of my face that exists for me, as at my birth, and all through my life

When young, however, I covered it over with the health of youth and it seemed to melt away to others when I smiled, though it remained concealed underneath Now nothing else existed for me I looked foreign to myself I was so unfamiliar with my looks I looked at a picture of myself and was surprised that this was me I did not see myself in any way that others did

DREAMS

"A bird started to hatch from its egg and its head came out wet, ugly and black Then it flew up, then down, to bite my right hand, I screamed and woke up"

Many of us actually dream while we are awake We forget when it is unpleasant or making no sense to us Dreams are childhood history You need to know a lot about a person before you can interpret his/her dream

When I was able to have dreams, they were so wonderfully revealing to me - that is how I could learn about myself best They were my truest teachers They were always telling me things, which caused me to give up on people And it seemed to me, that there was always some basis of truth in these critical dreams

Mother Animal

It was getting very dark and I was alone in the abandoned forest, near our farm I could hear the tramping of wild animal's feet. I was terrified I heard sounds like animal hoofs I found myself in a cave-like enclosure with a mother animal that was feeding live worms to her young I was in the opposite corner and wondered what I would do when she would come over When she did she offered me some worms to eat, and I felt a little safer, I realized I would have to eat it

I was in the cave waiting, waiting for what? To be fed, so that I could begin living? I was waiting for people who did not love me to love me If I waited, I would be fed, smiled

239

at, petted into believing what was not true I had waited for everyone Waiting did not work

Idiot Child

It is a mistake to look for hope outside oneself I dreamed that I had a child, and even in the dream I saw it was my life The child was an idiot and I ran away But it always crept back onto my lap again Until I thought, if I could kiss it, whatever was in myself, perhaps I could sleep So I went to its broken face It was horrible but I kissed it I thought I must finally take my own life in my arms

Lotto Tickets

I used to buy quite a number of lotto tickets and imagined I could or how I might win with one of them Whenever I bought lotto tickets and thought of the possibility of a win, I would dream of being in a room where I was in danger Some men were in this room looking for something I would have terror dreams They were in my apartment threatening to kill me, demanding my tickets I would give them the tickets in my dreams and I would wake with anxiety and relief I found it too unpleasant to possibly win and be hated for it so I stopped playing the lottery

Or the time I dreamed I was with my brother and he was gone and I was by myself I was carrying a small black purse In it I had three lotto tickets and a small radio I found myself in a room with some people and I lock the door to feel safe I then saw the look in their eyes and I almost cried, feeling sorry They were about to kill me and I didn't know why, as if it was some mistake, mistaking me for someone else? I was aware I should not have barred the door I had great fear and wondered how to get out I then found myself in the next room I saw my things being examined Some things were missing from my purse including the lotto tickets

Father Vs Husband

It was my childhood loneliness that followed me everywhere, all the time What made me feel good? When I thought about deciding to marry, I kept on having dreams of abandonment In the dreams I couldn't find my mother My father had left because he couldn't wait for me My father appeared as a symbol of my husband It made him too anxious and hostile to wait for me And although I was very quick, I deliberately kept waiting to see if he would wait And he did leave in the dream And I felt sorry for myself but I couldn't do anything about it

Name Card

Another dream was about my first husband I decided to give up on him and left him I was perhaps on the beach and he asked me to write my name on a card, which had writing on it I wrote my first and maiden name and then looked at the writing and realized with great fear that the card contained a story of a wife being killed by her husband, maybe by drowning, and I tore up the card with my name on it, as if to void permission of the act

Pushed Out Of Window

A dream about my second husband, I was aware of his emotional problems to some extent and I dreamed of him pushing me with his shoulders out the window, but if anyone he was the first person I've known who would save me except when he was destroying himself in his mood swings

Twenty-One Daughters

I recall a dream about my second husband where we went to visit his ex-family He showed no interest in his ex-wife or in all his young children-girls I counted twenty-one of them They were all friendly towards him and they all went with him on a sled towards the river, and he tried to push them in I stopped it and then he tried again to push me out the window with his shoulders, and I realized he was insane, and he admitted he tried to kill me too He yelled that he would still get me so that he could get the four and a half million Dollars I got away and passed through many people, and felt again that now I had no one, and that I must write to Irv But then I saw again his failings and I thought of Arthur and his failings too I could feel myself tightening my neck and teeth like my father, thoughts of my father's craziness and my own which must be related to my fear of my father, fear of his anger and my controlling myself I felt fear of being killed by anyone

Making Out

I was looking for a pretty dress to put on in another room Art was in the other room on the couch Gene came in as I walked into the other room and kissed Art on his mouth I expected him to push him away but surprisingly he accepted the kiss Then as I searched for the dress, I heard a loud licking noise and looked in, and saw Gene was at the foot of the couch, with Art's legs apart and Gene licking him. I couldn't find the pretty dress and felt it was no use looking pretty Art came in and said to me it didn't make him like me any the less just because he also liked this, that it changed nothing

Leg Operation

I had an operation I had on my leg, and during it they decided to remove part of the inside I felt I had not been told before and that no other doctor had been consulted I was told that they didn't know they had to remove parts of it before the operation and it was too late since it was started It was on the lower part of the leg I wondered, as I was awakening, why I had forgotten of the operation and I tried to remember it

Rope And Comb

When I was misdiagnosed and told by doctors I would die but miraculously recovered I kept on having this repeat dream of a rope and a comb that got pulled out of me, and fear of letting it go out completely So it stayed there all imbedded and rotting away

Daydreams

Many people talk about having fantasies, and when they do, they seem to mean having sexual fantasies My fantasies, daydreams, are very different I had fantasies about reading

Orphan Asylum

I daydreamed of living in an orphan asylum People feel sorry for children in orphan asylums and want to do things for them and give them all sorts of things I imagined I would live in a nice house where only children lived, and where nothing was demanded of them or expected of them and I could just read all the time

Insane Asylum

When everyone in my family worked all the time and I did not, and thus I was not meaningful, because all I wanted to do was to read During adolescence, I thought if I went insane, I would be locked up in a nice house, get fed without struggling for it, and some people would even feel sorry for me as they did for people in institutions I would be able to just read and read and read And, I thought, in case I wouldn't be considered crazy enough, I could become a nun and I would be required to be educated and expected to read all that and even be appreciated for it I had learned that books were friends

Prison

Sometimes I thought I might be innocently accused of some crime and would therefore be punished and sent to jail and being locked up all alone in my tiny cell And I would then have a nice place to live in, get food without working for it and I would be free to just read and read and no one would care or be around to stop me

Losing Feet

I had a fantasy of losing my feet so that I would not be able to do physical activities expected of me and so I could only read and write I was hoping that it would help me understand my problems within the family I started sitting a lot and not wanting to move

LEARNING TO BE OLD

If there was anything I knew well, it was the misery of life It wasn't that I myself had known only misery I had lots of good luck Yet I felt all of one's misery If I didn't feel it was my own I still felt that of others If there was anything I noticed wherever I might have been, it was not the geography, the home, not the way people were dressed, nor how they looked But it was any misery that existed there, anywhere This was my area of knowledge, my area of intelligence I felt the need to weep, not only for myself, but also for humankind To really be a human was not easy

Now coming to the end of life, I thought the problem of animal survival needs the survival of the fittest and what fittest was referring to - it was often the opposite where the fittest was often the destructive force of humankind

A gangster of today or a Spanish Conqueror survived by destroying others and stealing what the now dead people worked and created It was like the fittest of the destroyers against the fittest of the minds of others

Perhaps many people who look like humans are not The greatest human flaw and handicap is jealousy I had known retarded people who were real people and some highly educated and intelligent ones who were incapable of being real people Learning to be old is not very easy You find yourself that way without any previous experience or even education And you feel deserted by everyone who left you.

Very rare people are able to teach what they have not experienced Can it be that retarded people might make the best teachers for this since they know what it is like not having developed as far and are not frustrated by losing what aging does – going back to what we once were Infants learning to walk, they fall to learn but it doesn't work that way anymore Because now falling is no longer safe as it was in childhood Maybe each person just has to learn every new law and manage the best they can and just suffer the consequences

RIGHT OR WRONG

I sometimes don't know when I'm right and when I'm wrong. There have been times when I couldn't be sure that I might not be paranoid or the other person whom I put my trust in Under these circumstances, how can I make decisions? Then I just do nothing Can this be called wanting to eat your cake and having it too? Whatever I do is wrong to someone How can other people feel so absolutely right all the time? I seem to be never right to my family

At times I'm certain I am right and I can see what is wrong and what is right in the way other's think And then it just breaks down and I can't be sure of anything or of anyone, and I just go on, days passing, years passing

When people are sure of one side of something (in advising me about something) and I show them the other side, they are sometimes convinced that the other side is right Each time they are convinced, they have come to the correct decision But I become all the less convinced when I see how their thinking can be changed so easily by my misgivings

Because by then I would see how in their minds one thing is absolutely correct and then the opposite is also - each time the one side is seen and then the other disappears for them, is completely negated It is like the figure and ground kind of thing

PART TWO

Foreword

Paying My Debt

To this day, I don't understand why criminals pay their debt to society by going to jail They certainly don't pay by having others pay taxes to support them Who in society gets paid? It seems to me that society pays the debt that they owe If society is owed a debt, then why make society pay twice? If the criminals are to make a real payment, what kind of payment should they make?

Well, this writing is my payment I too owe a debt, a debt for being silent I never stood up for my rights I don't want to be known Fear of being hurt is at least one of the reasons why some people write fiction, and even when it is not fiction, they can say it is

Preface

About Part Two

I write negatively – satire and humor - subjective rather than objective, values and ethics rather than plot itself and about people and ideas rather than things

Introduction

History Repeats Itself

We actually have no laws because they are reinterpreted by the social prejudices of the times If we have no fixed morality but have a fluctuating one that changes according to social and political and other prejudices then why pretend we have law? The U N was supposed to be the hope of the world and is what?

Capital punishment is seen as uncivilized because the state must murder the murderer Cannibalism was accepted by society as cultural because it used to be that sometimes it was done out of need to avoid starvation

Perhaps someday we will accept murderers as being guiltless if they will eat their victims again?

Youth started to worship the ignorant, the criminal, thus the age of the hunter has returned The hunting instinct of man has returned in some of the young, since they are not allowed by the child labor laws to work, to struggle, thus they are returning to hunting And since there are no wild animals in the cities to hunt and to make them feel powerful and needed, these young now choose to hunt human prey

Since not all humans prey live outdoors, the hunt has extended to inside the homes All the laws of hunting apply here - such as the physically defenseless are sought. Will we have to use predatory animals to help hunt the human hunters, with hunting dogs to track them down in order to clear city forests, and city jungles in tall buildings?

While theoretically we don't have the right to be ignorant of the law - in the courts, anyway - we do have the right to be ignorant otherwise This is what makes our political parties so expensive and wasteful Because when it comes down to having the privilege and right to vote, our prejudices and wishful thinking is what does our voting for us, with almost any excuse as proof

The right to be stupid is what we get and what then follows is our right to blame others for our wrongs and non-thinking This is what destroys what is good in our civilization, and we all suffer from this as a result, and without realizing why

Society And Evolution

Evolution And Social Grouping

Just as some animals are greater predators, the killing qualities of some animals are more prevalent in some human species Animals have to abandon their offspring when a newborn is expected to leave, and be on their own

Early men were prey as well as predators The hell they went through in their evolution, for survival Human predators destroyed their ancestors by killing them for food

Hunting with weapons predated man Our precursors hunted so we evolved as man We must have used primitive weapons

Speech began with hunting and a human kind of social organization Hunting involves weapons, which require manufacturing of weapons Use of tools requires teaching and teaching requires language and capacity for organization

When males hunt and females gather the results are given to the children and rest of the family When the birth of our conscience occurred, our memories led to tradition, and tradition led to religion

The weapon fathered man He raised the animals - all are evolutionary products of the success of the hunting adaptation Agriculture has dominated human existence for less than one percent of man's history Man became man because of his years as a hunting animal Therefore it created the desire, even the need and certainly the emotion to destroy life as it came in the original package Killing is part of man

Man - with his upright position, his opposing thumb, and his pushed in face The result is that man has the adrenalin of a hunter and the digestive system of a herbivore We have to cook our meat to break down the proteins

When we are young every living thing becomes an educative toy Even a Siamese kitten, scores of generations removed from necessity, cannot resist killing a mouse, even though it will not eat it The same happened with our young man-ape play trying to copy adult activity

Boys have interest in hunting, fishing, fighting and games of war, which they developed in play At some point, grown men started killing for fun, from necessity to recreation

Sports can be seen as a ritualistic physical prowess Religion can be seen as a reutilization of fear Warfare with predators is society endorsed Hunting is now sports We were born with eyes, heart and brains of slayers, and as killers we live

Is it any wonder that man loves to kill?

Cannibalism Exists

It may be that evil is related to cannibalism, still as part of our early history Cannibalism still exists in various ways, not only in humans actually eating each other, as originally for survival

History has grown on lies Just as disease feeds on germs, Cannibalism is the original method of life for survival The big fish eat the little fish, some animals eat other animals and humans eat animals Those that eat other animals or those then eat plants And worms nourish on plants etc

There are other forms of symbols of cannibalism that involve tearing into those whom one is jealous of and though removed directly, are symbolically evident

A more extreme example of cannibalism is the German cannibal Armin Meiwes, who was arrested involving a victim, who had responded to his advertisement, wanting to be such a victim He received more than 200 responses of others who willingly offered themselves as victims

The past history of mankind is closer to some of us genetically more than to others This can explain so much of genocide, history, and what is not understood

Pecking Order

The natural pecking order of whole groups, one race against another is automatically a pecking order, and therefore gives the individual a natural pecking order

If those children come in contact with a different

cultural background and are taken out of their normal pecking order

Natural rank and dominance among individuals can be completely interfered with by the imposition of laws over the individual dominant rank by the government The higher and lower degrees of dominance by laws, the arm of the government occur in schools and in the family

Laws are artificial and unnatural restraints of dominance among people Since the government is and has to be in the first rank of dominance, so weaker ranking people can borrow the dominance of government thru the laws and oppose or overwhelm the dominant – and thus it is as if the house comes falling down

A couple of white hunters can go through Africa with some guns and successfully oppose the dominant (primitive)

Dominance comes into play constantly and is opposed by many things Money buys power and allows people to overcome natural dominance of others Ideas, culture, religions, ideologies, dogmas can frequently vitiate the normal and natural pecking order in complex societies

In primitive societies there is no interference with the normal pecking order causing frustration

Question Of The Century

What is the question of the century? It is not about the economy Not about the progressive political party It is not the conservative party It is not about the wasteful expenses that are not covered It is not about what we would imagine it is, it is the question of how are you Just observe the different answers of the question How are you? It is behind the question that the answer lies what is causing the lack of knowing how are you

Communication

To communicate requires more than language, more than really listening It requires how the other person thinks, and being able to follow and accept the irrationalities and peculiarities, and possible history, and not negate but to accept It is so easy to sometimes say something that even surprises the one who says it It is easy for a very truthful person to say something that is incorrect and suffer the consequences of an incorrectly spoken remark or to make a misunderstood statement that though correct and well intentioned, is interpreted very wrongly

The New Meaning Of Words

I still have difficulty understanding the new meaning of words Like "How are you?" Is now not a question but means a form of hello For me it is still a question, but I have finally learned to accept it by answering "Yes, thank you" And the questioner seems to accept it as if I answered, which I didn't

Retarded children are now called exceptional in schools It seems to be tied up with the high payments given to "teachers" of these children that are not only not exceptional but their teachers are even less exceptional

Well similarly with our dining room workers, it is with the word rare, which is misunderstood by them, and I keep wondering what is the new word that I do not know? When I asked for liver, I asked could I have it very rare? She said of course you can, and that is what you will get I didn't know the new word so what I got was a scorched dried out inedible liver When she placed it on the table in front of me, she proudly said "This is what you wanted, it is very rare" When I left I asked the one who acts as the head, what the correct word for very rare was She laughed and said she will find out. I decided while she is not finding out, and never will, I must wait until I learn the correct word before ordering it again

Where do these new meanings come from?

The same applies to politicians who are regressive but they call themselves now progressives Can it be that the new politicians create them? Do the old words mean the opposite of what the new words mean? If this is the answer, then I must ask for it scorched when I mean rare That is an easy answer if that is correct

Poor doesn't mean what is not even known today Poor often means less than some, sometimes more than many non-poor, and sometimes just not rich as the richest

Intelligent often means knowing how to makeup very big lies while smiling charmingly

Copying Advertisement And The Truth Lost

Copying advertisements, truth gets moved further and further away until it gets lost

Language helps to do this by changing the meanings of words Words that meant what we know they were changed to be the opposite Like retarded is now called exceptional and regressive is called progressive We make bad meaning good when they are not

This keeps on until we have only confusion And to most people good becomes bad and bad becomes good Some people use their religion to help with the lies We then regress to the times before scientific proof of facts when we simply believed only what we liked to believe and what we wanted as being the real truth for everyone And when this occurs within the government, it then teaches the people to do the same

Suppose all advertising were abolished? Would there be more honesty about products?

The World Has Become An Advertisement

The world has become an advertisement It is in, and by, newspapers, television, in our mail, in just everything It is so prevalent that I can't always recognize information that is not meant to be an advertisement

Since advertising does not have to be the absolute truth, but is expected to have embellishments, exaggerations, etc in order to show up what you want to get across The same methods of expression become part of our language and thinking

I wondered how all the ads could sound so alike to me as if one person made them all up for everyone and for everything It seems to me, that instead of their being what used to be, a one God for all religions, there has now developed instead a one God of, and for advertising

Real People

When I call on the telephone, I first have to ask "Are you a real person?" to know if I am talking to a recording of "one message fits all"

I am truly surprised when I find out I am actually hearing a real person I am so impressed that I just spill over with friendliness, as if I just found my true soul mate

If that doesn't happen - or before I discover it to be a real person - I never know what I might say - and I do say all sorts of things that I would not say if I knew To know what I said would surprise me more than anyone else

I do not know how different I become when I am talking to a non-person When, and if, the real person gets my message, I have no idea if anything was understood I do not even know if it was heard or listened to

Since the real person is used to not being real, he, she, or it doesn't feel the need to be real to answer anyway After experiencing the joy of being a recording, and not having to be there – at least not there to listen - and if heard, or even listened to - he, she, or it, is not there for answering Being so used to not being real-'it' now no longer feels the need to be real anymore

Obesity - Past And Future Evolution

Obese human beings have been discriminated against, and sometimes still are But I believe this may be an evolutionary stage, with the result that skinny people will become discriminated against in the near future, especially the ones that remain small. Some are already feeling they are, or can be stepped upon since people are becoming so tall and big The big people are much too strong for the customary frail sizes to compete with

I became frighteningly aware of this when I was squashed against a very sturdy heavy gal sitting next to me in an auto when her arm merely brushed against me, and it felt painful, as if a very heavy iron bar was weighing me down, and I felt afraid I thought if we would have an accident, that before getting killed by the accident, I would be crushed to death by her falling against me

We seem to be returning to past history in many other ways, and at the same time we may be going back to the time of Buddha, when part of his superiority was his obesity, which at that time was considered divine

Since the majority of people are developing great strength in their height and width, and majority attitudes and ideas become the norm, this may happen very soon

I have no idea how, but it will change our understanding of biology and medicine, certainly change our understanding of what is good for us, what is healthy, that is now considered not healthy It will influence new beliefs in medicine when doctors will tell us what we should do to abolish old concepts of aging

Bones especially are stronger in these people of the future, and even now Already developed - evolved so that many of today's problems regarding such fears will be wondered at, and believed to have been alleviated by new imaginary medical concepts

People Believe In The Idea Of Equality

People believe in the idea of equality But - equality of what? Do you know? Are people born the same? Why not? Do you want everyone to be the exact same as you? Do you like everything about yourself?

Do you want everyone to be better or worse than you are? Or the way you were born, or the way you have become?

Money And Equality

There is a common, philosophically childish belief that if everyone in a society had the same amount of money that it would then make people equal Many people really believe that rage, hatred, and all crimes are caused by poverty and that by eliminating poverty we will cure all evil people and evil behavior They ignore the reality that many people of wealth commit crimes, and that many very poor never do

People who believe that money is the cure of all evil in society also believe that having equal amounts of money is what makes people equal They ignore the fact that no person can possibly be equal to another, that all people have differences, both by birth and by experience It would also displease them immensely if everyone were exactly the same as themselves

Most people seek someone or something to blame, instead of seeking rational solutions for dissatisfactions, in order not to feel like the helpless infant that was completely dependent on others good intentions for survival. This infantile error for adulthood is always seeking a scapegoat, and is a serious part of inequality

It is inequality of justice, of fairness, to each other, beginning very early within the family, and remaining fixed in our unconscious, which then continues outward onto all others from then on It is the inequality of justice and rationality that makes people unequal in the most meaningful way

Money does not correct this inequality. In fact, many people with lots of money use their money to create more injustices Throughout history, they have often been the ones who have waved the banner of poverty to create the most and greatest injustices, and this continues to go on and be so

People continue to believe that poverty is the cause of all evil, and therefore, money is the cure of all evil The terrible things that some people do to others is often excused and blamed on poverty This is a historically continuous lie It is not that poverty does not exist The poor I have known never advertised it, as many not so poor do The truly poor do not look as if they were bursting with excessive energy, as the now called poor do

People who believe that money is the cure of all evil also believe that having equal amounts of money is what makes people equal. They ignore the fact that no person can possibly be equal in all ways to another All people have differences, by birth and experiences, as well as, circumstances and knowledge

Not only is the causal excuse of poverty used, but also the twisted use of fairness, as a fault created by society and its responsibility to correct, by equalization of wealth alone, calling that fairness Poverty often brings cooperation Jealousy, privatized or socialized, is the Achilles heel If everyone were poor, we as a human race could never do so much evil We would have to use our energies to forage for food and children would be happy to be of use, instead of just playing and having open mouths to be fed like birds without hands if the poverty is the fault of the rich, would poor people be rich if there were no rich people?

The Flag Of Poverty

Poor people like these don't usually ask, let alone demand, anything. They try to better themselves by their own efforts, instead of using their energy to reproduce future criminals and those who enjoy forever using the flag of poverty Justice vs Law, how each criminal acts could be compensated for, by the most just correction of it

The education of the distortion of history. A terrorist, a dictator, a thief, a destroyer of all that is good is honored as if he were a hero at his death and the world sends its representatives to honor him with dishonest praises Praising evil by all who mistake it for diplomacy

DNA existed before civilization We live in the future and feel guilty about the past We must be in the present to change the future and the past The root of any sickness equals the blocked light in an area, the life force of God We have to contact the energy The desire to change is the important need We are all inter-connected We are never alone Jealousy is the worst Evil eye means taking the energy from the other person We need to create a shield where negativity can't get through to protect ourselves Words have consciousness, a solution that is complicated can't be true Energy cannot disappear

Poverty often brings co-operation, unless there is jealousy. Jealousy, privatized or socialized is the Achilles heel If we were all poor, we as a human race could never do so much evil We would have to use our energies to forage for food And children would be glad to be helpful instead of just playing and having open mouths to be fed like birds without hands

Most human beings seek a scapegoat, someone or something to blame - instead of seeking solutions for dissatisfactions, and not to feel helpless and completely dependent on others for survival This irrational infantile error in adulthood is always seeking a scapegoat This is the most serious part of what creates inequality It is the inequality of real justice, of real fairness, to each other - beginning very early within the family, which continues outward onto others from then on It is this inequality of what is fair and just that makes people unequal in the most meaningful way

Money does not correct this. In fact many people with

a great amount of money use their money to create more injustices Throughout history, they often have been the ones who have waved the banner of poverty to create the most and greatest injustices.

The Nouveau Riche And The Nouveau Poor

We used to speak only of the "Nouveau Riche", never expecting that the poor could change very much as to be classified as old or new types. Poor people were classified as just always poor as if it were an unchangeable inherited reality Today, however, we have not only the nouveau riche, but also the nouveau poor

The old poor never looked as well fed and strong as the new poor of today The classic poor used much of their energy to forage for food, the new poor use much of their energy to forage for sex and fun, like some of the old riche and most of the nouveau riche do

Today the "Nouveau Poor" can't imagine what it is to be like the old poor In those days their children did not wait around to be entertained while being cared for And just like the poor used to work for the rich, today many people, including the government, now work for the "Nouveau Poor"

The "Nouveau Riche" used to be looked down upon by the old rich when there were not so many of them. Today even the classic, inherited rich have accepted and combined with the new rich in similar behavior and friendship, especially when it comes to entertainment and finances

A great many of the "Nouveau Riche" are entertainers. The newest, therefore the "Nouveau Nouveau Nouveau Riche" are those who entertain by playing games of ball.

Some other "Nouveau" are outside of the social scene so far because they entertain and are entertained more privately, with the new technology

We hear of terrible and evil things going on - all explained away by the word "poverty" It's not that there is no such thing as poverty, but the most really poor I have known never advertised their poverty as they do today

If more people were poor today – like during the great depression - there would be less crime and theft and envy as we have today. It is increased by the advertised belief that poverty by itself is the cause of all problems – when poverty actually brings more co- operation and kindness and sympathy, instead of jealousy

The "Nouveau Poor" have now become a model for reference, and glorified almost into a new kind of religion Poverty has become the new scapegoat to blame for everything, and has even been made by some into a new kind of messiah that has to be hanged and crucified in order to then be worshipped and blessed - before the new creation of the world of Love

How To Get Paid Well For Being Stupid

I have always been told that "Ignorance is no excuse before the law," but I have been finding out that this does not apply to everyone This is the way it was proven to me that stupidity is not against the law for everyone

For example, this sweet woman who loves to get a nice big full cup of hot coffee for her breakfast as she quickly rushes off to work in her auto mobile What better place to put it than on her lap between her legs so that her quick moving car can splash it around a bit and prove that it is full by spilling over into her lap (I do wonder if she teaches her children to do it like that?)

Not a stupid enough thing to do, she finds a lawyer who loves stupid people The kind of lawyer who loves to pick a stupid jury, especially those who hate people and companies richer than themselves, although they love the product the company sells The result is that the jury awards the woman millions of dollars for being stupid Rewarded so very well for her stupidity, don't you think?

Now I am wondering if such a jury who knows how to blame others for their own stupidity still loves this woman whom they made rich? Or do they now hate her too for being richer than themselves?

Not All Dummies Are The Same

The Dummy books are a great idea and have become big business because there are so many of us, especially when you combine the genuine dummies with the intelligent dummies.

Some of these books are not so easy to understand because some are written for the intelligent dummies, at least in part, or maybe even written by the intelligent dummies This is too bad because then you have to be one to understand one

There are many differences between the genuine dummies and the intelligent ones For instance, genuine dummies know what they know and know what they don't know. They don't have to fool themselves or anyone else

Intelligent dummies are not like that at all They think they know everything and they always think that what they know is correct, especially when it is not

Intelligent dummies are in the forefront everywhere In the stores, answering the telephones, in businesses, in schools, in the professions, and esp. in government agencies They are the dispensers of information and the ones who answer your questions They make up answers to questions in order to be polite and make you feel at home They sound as if they really believe their own answers, which they have just made up

They can even pretend they don't hate you when you question their answers They are experts in knowing how to pretend they know it all In a way, they decide what your questions ought to be because very often they really answer their own questions rather than yours And finally you realize they can't understand your question at all, and you must accept that as the final answer

The best thing to do is to answer your questions yourself Some genuine dummies do that well naturally having escaped the hazards resulting from education and training. This is how the saying "a child shall lead you" was born The wonders of it are that some genuine dummies remain that way instead of outgrowing it and becoming an intelligent dummy.

Children's Minds

We have been raising a generation of grown people with children's minds and memories without rational judgment They remain children in their minds

The helpless infant that was completely dependent on others for their good intentions for survival This irrational infantile era for adulthood is always seeking a scapegoat. This is the most serious part of what creates inequality

Not To Be Mistaken For Grown-Ups

There is such a fear of being mistaken for grown-ups, that they even conceal from themselves the fact that very small children are also grown-up in many ways In my day it used to be that older people really believed that small children had no feelings and no mind at all In fact, I used to have to pretend that they were right, not to embarrass them, and so I acted as sexless and as mindless as I was expected to Now that it is known and expected that they do feel and think, the children themselves try harder than ever to hide this as soon as they start showing signs of growing up

At this time, in spite of all this, there are some very small ones who refuse to go along with being either good or even being children, and they play the opposite kinds of games They do everything possible to prove what mature thieves and killers they can be, and they show the old people even how to have sex I'm not sure if they do this merely to have fun and play, or also to help teach them

Advance Or Regression

In trying to understand some of the present changes, I wonder if it's meaning is evolutionary advancement or just an adjustment to what has happened and what is

It used to be that people wrote poems to expose a thought or feeling Today it becomes a song and is expressed by the jumping up and down Is the jumping due to crowding or some evolutionary reason I don't know yet Is it is done in a form of aggressive expression? Is this aggression or exercise? People want the government to replace their parents? Is this an advance or regression of physical growth or emotional?

Change

Young people want change expecting change always to be better Change occurs whether you like it or not The most difficult thing is to change oneself

When we are very young is when we are formed and it is very difficult to change later on in life

Society And Psychology

Einstein

I wonder what Einstein thought when people who were less intelligent said to him that he is intelligent?

Maybe just like the dinosaur that became too complex and died off, maybe that is what is happening to the human being

Now The Insane Are The Sane

People do not know who is sane and who is insane So some years ago they decided to let everyone out of the asylums

Now the insane people have all the answers They say let us decide and rule So now the insane are the sane and are able to accuse and blame the others for everything that is wrong

Normal People, Geniuses and Idiots

Some normal people are crazier than crazy people are

Some examples Two small boys playing with their sheet

of white paper, which they then folded and called guns, for which the normal school authorities punished them by expelling them

When another small boy in grade school pulled an attractive little girl's curls, he was accused of sexual harassment Before schools became this normal, that was considered a form of teasing and admiration for the little girl

Normal people often consider geniuses crazy and crazy people are often considered normal by normal people When normal people think that crazy people are crazy, they like to punish them for it

There are also brilliant idiots This very intelligent and highly educated N Y lawyer, who is also heard over the radio, is a truly brilliant defender of irrationality To a great many people, irrationality is normal

Successful Relationships

Successful relationships depend more on how curious the partners are than on how smart they happen to be. Also if both are non-curious, then I Q also does not matter Like-mindedness attracts and opposites repel in long term, but in short- term, relationships can be physically attracted

Incompatibility

I must be asking myself wrong questions - since it can't be answered simply enough The question of who is evil It may be that when two incompatible people live together they both have to be evil to each other I am evil when I allow myself to be abused, used, made unhappy and for staying around and putting someone into the position of wanting to behave evilly toward me Perhaps we must act evil to each other in order to live together Perhaps just the fact that there are such divergent personalities that exist with different needs and different ways of thinking is what creates evil behavior For in some cases there is no other way of coping with extremely different types of people, different species, coping with each other, often even in the same family, even between parent and child

Jealousy

Jealousy is the greatest motivational aspect of human beings, next to survival, and often even supersedes it When this happens, it even works against survival. It is much more destructive than other inherently damaging attributes of human nature

Jealousy motivates everyone in endless ways - and is a driving force in life - both constructive and destructive Since it is more often destructive, it is important to be able to recognize its danger

In my experience, when others may delight in knowing that others feel jealous of them, with me. I felt it was necessary, (and I was willing), - to eradicate bits of myself- to help others not feel this way about me in order for me not to be afraid of them

Sex As Part Of The Digestive System

Some people really think that sex is part of the digestive system. Most male persons really believe that for a female person to like him at all, she must show it by instant sexual feedings

They act as if science were wrong and the heart does not lie in the heart area, and that the mind does not lie in the mind area, but that the heart and the mind lie in the sexual area, and of course, that the sexual area is part of the digestive system

Smoking And Public Sex

Smoking is like public sex You can't smoke without making others smoke your smoke, just as you cannot get excluded in the presence of public sex Both smoking and sex invades all who are present

Looking For A Matchmaking Heart

I met a lady through a mutual friend, and I was invited to her home It was a beautiful day, a beautiful beginning I was impressed with the others' elegance and her ability to express herself What a nice new friend!

After a long, very friendly, and very satisfying give and take, both interested in similar activities and work, by some accident our conversation touched upon political matters, exposing our different viewpoints.

The new friend was displeased to learn that I was not politically liberal like her She explained her preference to me by stating that liberals have a heart, and she demonstrated this by placing her hand over her own heart

She continued on to stress her ability of having a heart for people, and didn't want to hear anything further from anyone not having this same kind of heart If you are not politically liberal, you cannot have heart, you cannot feel for anyone

With the same hand with which she had touched her heart, she waved the no-longer-to-be-friend away Like a mosquito being chased away, I was no longer a human being to her, and she had no heart for me any longer

It was now apparent to me that I will never get to know what that kind heart was like, and the no- longer-friend who believed herself as absolutely right would never learn about me, not having her kind of matching heart

It is very sad that friendships – and even civilizations – can be destroyed by human emotions imbedded in childhood that are not remembered but remain influencing our lives forever

What We Think Affects The Body

Since what we think and feel affects our body, the mother's body is sensitive to receiving impressions Infants can tell how people react to them, if they are wanted or rejected A baby nursed on negativity receives the most poisons Parents do unto their children as was done to them, which they didn't want done

What the world is today hostility is raging. How negative and more powerful, 100 persons may enter the room and complement you and your first reaction may be amazement and self-consciousness, then a guilty pleasure You feel guilty for fooling them, because they don't know enough and because you know they don't really mean it But let one person be negative and you believe it

Doctors, Godlike Role Play

It is fear, not guilt, which is troubling, thus we are deprived of feeling healthy guilt, by not taking responsibility for rectifying responsible hurts to others To the child, and therefore to the unconscious, the physician pronounces death to what is bad

It's All Relative

There are different kinds of minorities, aren't there? Kings are minorities Murderers are minorities, or at least they used to be Saints are minorities

Are some minorities good and some bad? Or is everything relative? This relative thing is very interesting You can always change it by saying. "Oh, well its all relative" In that way we can change the meaning of anything

Do Roaches Have A Right To Live?

"Do roaches have the right to life?" I asked myself. It was a time when we were inundated with a particularly strong and very healthy, new variety of roaches in our city of N Y Roaches are intelligent, have a very long history that goes very far back before humans, are fully and beautifully formed, and functioning Right now, so many of them have chosen to live comfortably with me in my apartment, and eat at all my food

When they look me in the eye and run toward me rather than away from me, I feel guilty to kill them. So I talk to them and tell them "I do believe in your rights, but the problem is that you are taking away my right to privacy, as well as presenting me with risks because I do not know where you have been and with whom before me I tell them, "I'm willing to feed you if you allow me un-invaded space"

But I do not think they are concerned about my feelings because, if they were, they would not alarm me so with their exuberant multitudes If they weren't so arrogant, they could even avoid showing themselves to me, since they have endless hiding places

I do find it very difficult to see them as loveable and huggable And while I may also not be loveable to them, they make me feel that I am very huggable to them because they like to crawl onto my arm when I don't aggressively and hastily reject them

Dogs forgive, humans don't Dogs will risk their lives for their owner

Freud said a person can be in love with someone without

knowing it because of blocked access to his emotions, and the cause of human misery lay in the trauma of our childhood

Dogs feel more intensely than humans. Humans have ambivalence and can experience deception Dogs are without ambivalence

Society And Religion

The Idea Of God

God is used in trying to understand what is not understood, what is not known.

It is used in so many ways by different types of people as attempts to understand ones self, others, and all that is not known by different ways in the attempt to understand the unknowable, and to seek a principle of unity with others

The idea of God is to perceive an idea of the world It can be misused and expresses man's capacity for evil The mystery of God is the mystery of man himself

Do Christians Need Jews To Save Them?

I had heard a preacher on television say that the world will be saved when the Jews believe in Christ as their God - that is if Jews become Christians

Why is it that these Christians need Jews to save them? And no others? Why do Jews have to save Christians when Jesus has already saved them once? Why does this have to be repeated? And why must Jews take on the sins of Christians to save the Christians? What would then be expected if all Jews became Christians and still didn't get saved? What would then be demanded of the surviving Jews? If no Jews survived would that help the Christians?

I heard Russian communists say that in order for communism to work in Russia, the whole world has to become communists

And, if all Jews did become Christian to save the world, would the world become communists or would the communists become Christians due to the Jews having become Christians and having saved the world?

What Is A Jew?

A Jew is a person who is chosen Chosen to be the scapegoat of the world throughout history As a result, the Jew has been without a country, with a history of roaming from one country to another Depending on when the political or religious rulers need them and welcome them up to the times when they reject them, feeling they need them no longer

Similarly, more recently, it occurred to a Jewish doctor, whom Castro had considered very valuable until be decided that this doctor "knew too much", and he decided to have him killed (Cuban doctors in the Mercy Hospital told me this, but he was forewarned by someone, and was able to escape)

Similar to why the Romans had Jesus crucified It was the same with all the made up accusations against Jews throughout history After a ruler would pretend to offer

Jews freedom in order to get what he needed and wanted, he would then enslave them and begin their destruction It is a continuation of a form of cannibalism when eating the brains of the victim was the chosen reward

If Jews served no other purpose in world history, they would still serve the purpose of being the scapegoat for the entire world - a very convenient substitute for realizing their true dissatisfaction and hatred of themselves, of their parents, their rulers, or their Gods

At these times, they do not consider Jews human when they are alive, but then at times consider them Gods when they are dead When the country is in trouble they hallucinate that it is the Jews that are the cause of all their own unhappiness, even of all their own evil thoughts and deeds

A New York Times article states. 'In Poland, a Jewish Revival Thrives - minus Jews! Every June, a festival of Jewish culture is held to pay homage to the people who once lived there and contributed so much to Polish culture They sing Jewish songs and dance Jewish dances"

So you hate the Jews when they are alive, but how you love them when they are dead! Throughout history when a country has been in trouble, you invite them, and when they come and start to trust you, and because they do their best, you are envious and you murder and destroy them You pretend they have horns, that they take red blood – while you are taking theirs – and make white flat bread magically out of your red blood!

You have taken one of them, and not only made him your God, but then even made him non-Jewish, divorcing him from his religion, and claiming him as the beginning of yours You do everything to make Jews fear you when you mention his name You do this to always remind them of what you did to him and to so many of them, and are ready and able to continue to do so again

After murdering him, then you made sure to make them the victims, by teaching your lies everywhere, and continuing to tell your children, and those children to their children Teaching that he was not one of them, and that it was not you that had him murdered and that Jews must feel forever guilty for your deed by turning their other cheek to you so you can be ready to strike them again whenever it seems necessary or convenient so that your frustrations have someone else to blame for all human mistakes and unhappiness

It is very easy for some of you to forgive yourselves - all you have to do is say a few Hail Mary's' In a religion that expresses symbolically that wine is the blood and a wafer is the body of God, this is still the expression of past-inherited cannibalism that goes very far back as part of past survival

Because of this social cannibalism keeps getting continued by the use of Anti-Semitism Yes, Anti-Semitism is the result of inherited social cannibalism which recurs and recurs very strongly when problems of survival becomes problematical or questionable, and which occurs periodically whenever it gets caused by wrong political and economic choices, even when imaginative threats of survival occurs

Of course social cannibalism only begins with Anti Semitism, it does not end there, even though awareness is forever lacking

I Am "The Jew"

Blame the Jew! Blame the Jew! The Jew is at fault for everything that bothers you! I am that terrible Jew!

Are Jews a religion, a nationality, a race or none of these? Or is a Jew a Jew because a non - Jew considers him that? And is able to blame him for all his bad feelings? Perhaps many Jews would not have remained as Jews since they were without a country to defend them, often without a religion of acceptance, and certainly without being a single race!

Even people such as Vanessa Redgrave, and Gore Vidal, although they do not know me, hate me because I am a Jew If I am a Jew - what am I? Or am I what Vanessa Redgrave and Gore Vidal, say I am- only that I am a Jew

How many people know me? What I am is what they say I am, though they do not know me Do they even know what they themselves are? Do they think I am what they don't want themselves to be? Though they do not even know of my existence, they do know they are against me

Someone once told me that he could always recognize a Jew by looking at his eyes Is this a look of distrust, of fear, of pain? And what causes it? I also wondered why he told me that he could get a lot of money for his little daughter who was with him, because she is a Christian child in great demand He was an American moneychanger in South America, of German descent

The historic Edith Stein was born Jewish and converted to Catholicism, and as a devoted Catholic, was taken from the church to be murdered for having been Jewish, though she was a Catholic What is your explanation?

I Am The One You Hate

I am the one you hate for I am a Jew

In my memories are such as my first day in school I was a 6 years old child and it was my first day in school A boy in my class, his name was Lawrence, I can still remember his name after so many years, at the end of that first day, as I was leaving the school, he yelled "Jew Bastard" as he kept throwing stones at me, the way the religious Arabs do now in the Mideast

Every morning we pledged allegiance to the flag, to God, to the country, which I did, but to the vocal children, it wasn't my country or my God, even though I was born here and some of the others were not I felt like 'the man without a country'.

Several years later we moved to upstate New York, as I walked miles along the country road to grade school, and later to high school, I passed neighboring houses with signs "No dogs or Jews allowed" My brother has one of these wooden signs that he acquired somehow This area of New York many people today call the Jewish Catskills Actually it never was, except for two months in the summer when New York City people invaded the low priced summer resort types of getaways

We lived there all year and few other Jewish farmers like ourselves The Jews were summer people, and they supported the area, when it wasn't good enough for others Until much later when it achieved popularity that it was a bargain and before poor people became rich enough to travel

The New York City people never learned country behavior and never learned about the wooden signs

I remember well a lovely little girl who lived near the school we both attended - we became best friends At Easter she asked me to go to church with her during the Easter celebration My mother told me to respect all religions, and I would hurt her feelings by not going We sat together happily Until, at some point, the priest said that the Jews killed Christ My special friend never spoke to me again When we passed each other at school, she hung her head, and would not look at me

Jews Have Been Hated

Judaism expects and demands a greater maturity than many people are ready to accept It is much easier to reject this degree of maturity by hating the Jews for it

Jews believe that all people should take responsibility for themselves, and in self-blame Jews have been hated for this Today even very many Jews hate the Jews because of this They became accustomed to wanting things to be easier by turning to Christianity because it doesn't expect self- responsibility and self-blame

There is a famous old saying that "The greater the lie, the more it is believed, the greater the truth, the less it is believed

Not only did Hitler know and used this, so does our attractive president know and use it. Freud made a study of how irrational thinking works and why

Resented Because Of Their Talents

Lack of physical affection, a love of inflicting pain (Arabs) In England, at the time of Shakespeare, love of your kids was considered inappropriate "Spare the rod and spoil the child" The children tortured chickens, burned cats alive, and pitted animals against each other All this was fun Later humans developed love of sports. Arabs allowed men to hold hands but not with women - like most of us. The Moslems see only their good sides and not their dark impulses, see them as belonging in their enemies.

When someone does something bad - if he is a Jew - the news always mentions that it is a Jew, but never calls or mention that it is a Christian who has done something bad When a Jew does something great, they never mention that it is a Jew Never do they say Einstein the Jew, or Freud, the Jew When people resent Jews because of some talent, perhaps forced to develop for survival, when jealous, they should be told to get themselves persecuted and perhaps then they will do as well

The hardest thing about being a human is to understand what the others are and what they really mean rather than what they appear to mean, acting a certain way and not knowing what is inside- then hurts, their misunderstandings While you misunderstand them, they are also misunderstanding you, and then one misunderstanding builds upon another That applies to me and the pain is all that's left with me, and that grows and grows. If you don't get it right from birth, it keeps going wrong Those who deliberately give pain to others are more "Normal" and better off

Reverend Jessie Jackson is so holy that he doesn't need to use a toilet He defecates from his mouth Farrakhan's holiness, leader of the religious group Nation of Islam, however, consists of a super- human iron intestinal tract that converts his food into bullets and daggers, which he ejects from his mouth

Why Christians Hate Jews

Education was one of the principal reasons why the early Christians hated Jews Eighteen centuries ahead of the rest of the world, the Jews had compulsive public education Early religious commitment to literacy was the secret of continuing Jewish success and the source of consistent envy The Jews could carry their religious traditions with them into exile For the next two thousand years, the Jews were the only literate nomads on the face of the earth.

Literacy also allowed the Jews to develop a unifying sense of their own history The ability to read existed almost a century before Jesus was even born Every Jewish village was required to have a teacher to train young men to read religious scripture

An example, using the same wooden bowls for milk and meat products is a bad idea in the hot desert climate Therefore it was the first written public health code in the world, which appears in the Hebrew Bible, the Torah

The Ambassador Christian College states in one of their pamphlets "In the 14th century the bubonic plague struck Asia and Europe because of its poor sanitation The

Jewish physician Balavignus instituted a clean up movement among the Jews and the rats left the ghettos As a result the Jews mortality rate was less than its non-Jewish neighbors But instead of emulating the hygienic measures, its people accused the Jews of causing the plague and poisoning the wells and a general massacre was launched against the Jews! Balavignus was persecuted and tortured to make him "confess" that he was responsible for the disease!

Descendant Of Job And Abel

I am a descendant of Job and of Abel and often find myself surrounded and affected by the descendants of Cain His descendants are more abundant The world is mostly affected by the Cain's Some of them are mixed and are very deceiving (they are psychopaths) to those from Abel. Those are the descendants of Cain with their genetics and the spreading of mixtures of all the Cain's

Jews And Hitler

Referred to the bible as the monument history of mankind To cleanse his own soul Hitler saw himself as continuing the work of Jesus, the work against the Jews, as a Messiah.

People deny that Hitler was religious Himmler was even more religious, also Roman Catholic, which is religious practice of fundamentalism Hitler's mother had a strong faith and remained Roman Catholic

1945 May 6th mass held for him honoring Hitler, and the

church helped Nazis to escape to Argentina The church had cooperated with him and also helped and encourage anti-Semitism including Catholics who had Jewish ancestors

The Jew Jesus

Jesus has been persecuted over and over again in the form of other people

Whenever a scapegoat is needed, a Jew can be picked out to be the new Jesus - over and over again, the repetition of History

Some Americans have been demanding a new crucifixion – that the Jews be the victims for all immorality These Americans have been setting themselves up as the judges of morality to appease the more immoral demands of the judges who judge not themselves

As Rome of Yesterday, these Americans were and are demanding that the Jew be the victim of all immorality, cheekily demanding the Jew to turn his cheek, bullying the Jew into his roll of masochism, martyrdom

He feared only because he was anti Semitic He was obsessed with it, as his original sin that Jews were Satan-born

In John, the Jews are the children of Satan The snake symbolism of Satan struggle of power of church over state and words from New Testament attributed to Jesus by St Paul

Evolution Of Emotions

The evolution of emotions is not easily recognized when it turns into destruction of physical evolving The mind is able to find ways to deny reality and is able to not even connect the result with the cause Mostly this is a psychological way to avoid blaming oneself, not to see ones own faults and to avoid feeling guilt and finding excuses as if there were reasons for someone else's fault, thus putting the guilt on an innocent person or group away from oneself

Some of the early followers of Jesus, a Jew, were able to use the symbol of Jesus as if he were not one, in order to want to destroy all the others to feel superior

Christ, the Greek word for Messiah, became a symbol for their right to persecute the other Jews This need to make oneself feel superior is always connected with jealousy Many Jews also forgot the connection, and after endless persecutions began to symbolically identify the word Jesus with the cause of their deaths. However, today many Jews are able to realize that, in spite of the fact that the word Jesus for generations and generations meant swords and daggers against them, that by this time, civilization has gained and, to some extent, risen above it

Just as there are different degrees and changes evolving in different animals, so it is in human evolving Some children become more and more like the parents in accepting their negative traits, while some offspring learn from that and take on their positive traits, and fewer who are able to reject the negative destructive ones

When people began calling themselves Christians,

and had adopted parts of Judaism and mixed it with Pantheism, they began to persecute the Jews. Then many Jews even tended to forget that Jesus was one of them because symbolically he became the cause of their being persecuted He was not only murdered by the Romans, but the Romans, who then dared not to take the blame for what they did and called him God, then distorted history to turn the blame on the ancestors and descendants of Jesus Always most humans who are guilty or jealous find reasons to put the blame of their hurts and inadequacies on someone else

Just as a child who is neglected and mistreated by a parent turns its hatred against another sibling, and just about anything available, because the parent responsible is more necessary for its survival

Praying For Love Or Justice?

People pray for all sorts of things. If I would, or could successfully pray, I would pray for fairness, for justice I would rather have fairness than love Perhaps the word love is sometimes used as a substitute word for fairness?

I don't trust "love" All sorts of things are called love Desire is often called love Sex is usually confused with love Love often turns into hatred, and revenge

I don't think there can be love without fairness, without justice By justice, I do not mean to confuse it with equality To me, religion - at least my religion - is a matter of justice, nothing else It is something I do not experience very often in relationships with others It seems to me that all my life

I keep looking and waiting for, and falsely expecting it - as if it were my human right.

It is because of this desire, and expectation of justice, that I am chronically pained If I did not expect it, feel it as a need, I would be free of most frustrations and hurts I sometimes think I must be at fault for thinking this way

Today is Easter Sunday Christianity believes that Jesus died for other's sins In the same manner of thinking, I sometimes feel that I am at fault for other's wrong doing. That if I always knew the right thing to say, and do, then the people I know would not be at fault in their behavior, and would not suffer or cause suffering to others While I am aware of my unimportance, I apparently feel that I am important in this way as to be at fault for not being able to help others be more righteous and just

Most people don't like it, don't want it, and resent it - without realizing what they resent in me Even when a religion stresses this, it is also resented by those religions that do not.

In general I have been often resented more for my virtues, rather than for my faults. It would not be so bad if it weren't that I seem to mingle with such persons, by choice or habit or attraction? Of course all this starts very early in life and doesn't get turned off easily.

Some people call it Karma But the Yogi I once knew - when he was interested in me - told me I was an old soul - almost pure and ready to be complete, and therefore my last incarnation However, when he became disappointed by my lack of physical response to him - he then changed his thinking and said that I had to have had a terrible Karma to be experiencing my present life That is what I find "love" is about

At least I have had numerous destructive experiences relating to what is called "love" And many times merely because I, as the recipient, am either unaware of the other person's feelings or unable to return it in kind to all those in need, or desire, of it. In many cases, when love has not been returned the way the person wanted it, then extreme hatred follows with a vengeance

In the name of love so many abuses occur I wonder how many different kinds of things are classified as love?

Long ago I saw a foreign movie about a young girl living in a small agricultural town She was the prettiest, kindest, and wisest – and therefore greatly admired and loved by all In the end, people came forward and attacked her with their pitchforks She was loved and admired for all her virtues and hated enough to have to die for having these virtues Such is within human nature - and is one form of love

But back to the belief that Jesus died for people's sins - yes, he died because of people's sins, - not for them To think that he died in order to remove the sins of others is not only a perversion of rationality, but also the greatest example of true injustice

If this is not seen for what it is how can children be taught about justice when they are taught to believe something so irrational? And how can adults expect justice when they had been taught how to avoid it - by putting their blame where it does not belong?

Society, Politics And Economy

The Right And Wrong In Education And Law

When I attended Columbia University and took some courses at Teachers College, some professors who were teaching future teachers, insisted that I cannot- must not- judge anything as being right or wrong. Right and Wrong is only relative, they insisted, and is not to be judged

The teaching of right and wrong as erroneous started that long ago and has been influencing our present- day thinking and behavior

The law defines insanity as not knowing the difference between right and wrong Thus if insanity means not recognizing the difference - and at the same time, ideas should not be judged as right or wrong because ideas of morality are merely relative- then it follows that insanity is normal

If it is therefore normal not to know the difference because it is only relative - and at the same time the law judges insanity as not knowing the difference - then the result is the mental chaos which we have in our schools, in our streets, and in our homes

Education colleges concentrate on methods rather than content of truth, values, justice and fairness

How To Improve Our Education System

Even trying to improve our education system we must first start with justice and law. I have taught in public schools It is not the amount of salary that makes an education system good or bad Money is the least important factor in making or breaking education

Firstly, education for what? If laws, lawyers and judges and courts are not concerned with truth and fairness, that country cannot have truth in education Nor can it have respect from other countries Our laws are not concerned with justice What is justice?

With the present corruption and the so-called political correctness of lies which is extremely noticeable in politics, in advertising, and its influence in everything One of the overlooked influences on greeting with "How are you?" you are supposed to lie and say "great" or "good"

The "I love you" is another example I love you to death is more obvious about what might be meant by love Or "Sweetheart, my darling", perhaps it is said before it really becomes true Maybe this is a middle evolutionary step before it really becomes true

What Is Justice?

What is justice? Love others is preached everywhere Why is it that people have to be told constantly to love? Can a person love who does not know or understand justice?

Some religions have befogged and blurred the concept of justice The newspapers are full of concern for improvements, of elimination of juvenile delinquency and improvement of education

All problems are product of lack of truth and justice

The choices are only between justice and power. Where justice is not the first consideration, it must be power and might and ignorance

A society is only as good as it is just - not riches Factual and technical knowledge is very important but not enough Military strength is important but it is certainly not enough Education is very important but it is not enough for educated people can do evil more excellently

The right education, which has to include truth and justice, is the beginning after knowledge of what justice is

Social Worker's Paradise And Our Insanities

Our insanities have also changed Today we have the social workers paradise of insanities All the problems, if man will be cured by social workers, who will descend upon us from the moment we are born to guide us.

Human beings cannot be allowed to develop in the world by themselves They must be coddled from the day they are born by non- human super social workers and receive the advantages of the money the social workers will get for doing this

Parents are not to be trusted, and should be guided by social workers even if they too had parents The entire surroundings must be refashioned and reshaped and no expense spared because the money used will create superior knowledge and capabilities

All school dropouts can become social workers And everyone has the right to become president because that is the definition of Democracy

American Children

American children are brought up in a Democracy, which is known as the best of all, and have learned to associate it with the word democratic party They are unable to recognize evil Some are even very bored with everything being so much the same and want 'change' And to them change means of course even better So every one of them thinks more democracy is better than what they now have

However there are masses of people who hate, have been brought up from two years old to hate what American children were brought up to love The children brought up to hate are very intelligent in knowing ways of expressing their hatred For instance the muslins, as well as all non-democratic groups of people, understands that if they call themselves democrats, which will win votes This is so easy to do because so many people confuse Democracy with the words democratic party

Mass psychology does the thinking and irrationality wins The present Muslins learned that all they had to do was call themselves democrats and the White House is theirs Then they went further and said they want to work with the opposing people and they just sit by and wait for them to agree and continue its new democratic ruling by continuing to want to work out the disagreements with the others This "offer" consists of nothing but waiting for the others to agree, to get tired of waiting and coming to agree with them

Projection And How To Win

I was familiar with bullies such as destructive parents, children in gangs, criminal mobsters, and dictators who disallow and confiscate weapons of self-defense, etc

Of course lawyers who destroy justice for innocent people whom they damage by destructive verbal bullying in order to win

Only recently have I witnessed how our present government won over all rationality by the use of verbal bullying This method included the motto of the bigger the lie the more it will be believed Even Hitler acknowledged that he made use of this fact about human nature.

Freud called it projection Whatever you don't like about yourself, you see those traits in others who are not that way

What happened in Russia when the ruled became the rulers of the previously ruled, as well as the previous rulers? It is like making the children into the parents

What We Don't Like

It is common to not believe what you don't like So politicians use this and create more problems to civilization

In order to recognize people that lie and deceive, you need to have learned to lie yourself

If you do not lie you do not recognize if someone is not telling the truth

Whose Fault Is It?

Now, for instance if I have a sore foot and ride on a bus and someone steps on my sore foot, and it makes it worse –is this the fault of the bus company for being crowded, all the people inside the bus, or outside of it, or the person who stepped on my foot, or the fact that I had to use the bus? Or what caused him to step on my foot - the bus lurching, the driver, the bad roads and the way the bus was constructed? Or was it the man's attitude, his way of behaving, or the fault of the sore foot? Or was it God's fault, or society, or the local government? When a child throws a bottle out of the window and it hits someone, whose fault is it? Is the bottle company at fault, the parents for making the child, for having windows, and to have open windows?

The Right To Blame Others

While theoretically we don't have the right to be ignorant of the law - in the courts, anyway, we do have the right to be ignorant and stupid otherwise. This is what makes our political parties so expensive and wasteful

Because when it comes down to having the privilege and right to vote, it is our prejudices and wishful thinking that does the voting for us Finding some part that could be useful for oneself and using almost any such excuse as proof That is what our money gets used for!

The right to be stupid is what we get What follows then is our right to blame others for our mistakes in judgment This is what destroys what is good in our civilization We all suffer from the result, mostly without knowing why

Money Never Solves All Problems

American people still want to believe that money can solve all problems

The lesson by Russia has not convinced enough people that money is not the real solution for problems The American idea of creating the new "Great Society" by using (thereby misusing) money created more problems.

Now, when all the new "health benefits" will be enacted, we will learn that using money to solve everything does not work In fact, it can, and has, caused many more problems What is wrong with our present health-care system was actually created by using money as if that would solve everything - as a substitute for solving human problems By substituting lack of money as the cause for all problems, the need to understand human problems is abolished and forgotten

Then using money is the easiest to misuse and is causing endless more problems

We wouldn't have so much crime by children if they had

to learn how to survive hardships instead of learning how many luxuries some have - mostly useless

How To Balance The Budget
And Avoid More Prisons

Our government has been working so hard to find ways to increase productivity and employment Our President Clinton has even been traveling abroad in search for such a needed solution to stimulate our stagnant economy He has been unsuccessful so far except for diet pills, fertility pills, and anti-abortion pills

Our private sector has also failed to provide us with such a needed product due to its selfish concern about high taxes and regulations

I think that only a product, which is universally needed, could automatically solve all our economic, as well as social, problems today.

Everything can still be remedied if our President (preferably before election) would only recommend that our government instantly patent and manufacture a made in-U S.A, mechanical parent as a replacement for our present method of breeding children without parents (This method had been copied by us from the farmers' way of breeding chickens from eggs in heated brooders without the presence of the mother hen)

Our factories would soon be working overtime on making computerized loving parents with all the proper parental skills and all "Made in the U S.A." labels

It would even make our Unions very happy and minimum wages would simply explode by themselves

Our production of criminals would then be so reduced that the need for more prisons would be unnecessary, and the forever-increasing budget would get a well-deserved rest Most of our government officials could then go happily on vacations

The only resulting problem I can see is the jeopardizing of our Right of Freedom to do crime and spread falsehoods and that might create a serious problem for lawyers

Tipping Is A Contagious Disease

Tipping is a form of payment that is an offshoot of slavery. In my early days, and still engraved in my thinking - accepting, or even being offered a tip was something to be embarrassed about It felt like an insult To me it was akin to begging, bondage, or prostitution

While sometimes it can even be well deserved for a service, not otherwise compensated for, basically it is something that is not meant to be a true payment - and it usually is not - but is a kind of reward for either being pleased - or more often, pretending to be pleased In this way, it is not something earned but a reward for being satisfied - or even worse as a bribe - and which is much more common

Some people are appreciated more for giving large tips, while others who do not, may be even more appreciated

Some people are not appreciated no matter what they do In that way it is also an offshoot of gambling.

As bribes, it becomes inflationary, because bribes are never enough Like a fever, the more you do, the higher the fever Sometimes the bribe is given out of fear, to avoid being harmed in some way, similar to paying off a bully, or dictator Sometimes it is a form of advance payment for future favors

In addition to all that, it is like a contagious disease in that everyone has to catch it and pretty much outdo others in order to feel correct and worthy, or not be embarrassed and feel guilty.

Bush, The Real Serpent

In the past the serpent had to go all the way to the Garden of Eden to do its damage Today the serpent just keeps on smiling as he runs to the Internet and TV to do the same

But instead of a tree, he keeps saying "No, it's a Bush" He keeps repeating Bush, Bush, Bush, Bush! And they all cry back "Yes, Bush, Bush"

Bush then becomes the real serpent

Abortion Laws And Politics

It is interesting how little our politicians show concern about protecting people's lives from predators and yet fight so much to protect fetuses Can it be because we have so many laws protecting the criminals and murderers, that it is necessary to preserve possible fetuses in order to provide the predators with new populations for continuing their rights?

I don't like normal people - that is, normal in our society, I feel there is something wrong with them

Anti-abortion-People, who eat eggs are committing murder by not allowing the egg to hatch into a chicken

Obama, Our Last President Is A Successful Orator

Our president is a successful orator He is very active and attractive In his speeches he keeps saying the opposite of what he means, and he is believed because he keeps telling us what he knows we like to believe He is successful and admired for it

Our president is excellent in knowing how to keep blaming others because in that way he keeps others from blaming him

There is the famous old saying "The greater the lie, the more it is believed, the greater the truth, the less it is believed" Not only did Hitler know and use this, so does our attractive president know and use it Freud made an important study of how irrational thinking works and why

Mirror, Mirror On The Wall Who Is The Fittest Of Us All?

Proof for the theory of natural selection for the survival of the fittest is the criminal This fittest of all is not only well specialized in such abilities, but also familiar in all areas of survival so as to be able to constantly adapt to new changes to fit any new type of crime made available by evolutionary changes

Have you ever known of a time or place where criminals went out of style or ceased to exist? I have not The criminal seems to be born knowing how to survive off others, and therefore is always able to adapt to all changes by finding new avenues to fit new types of crime.

In my neighborhood the examples of this evolutionary phase is very noticeable and worth learning from To not be one of them is certainly dangerous and limiting to the survival of the unfit like myself

In fact, most of the people I meet are shifting little by little in that direction to escape becoming a victim To avoid non-survival, they have also begun to practice victimizing others, starting first with friends and relatives

I have a friend J, and to prove her good intentions and friendship, she showers me with feelings of guilt as to my unfitness The result is that I, an unfit, am becoming more and more in the outcast class, for lacking such fitness for survival

The way it looks to me right now, is that I am nearing my extinction proof that criminals are truly the fittest of us all because they are extinction proof

An Outlawed Subspecies

Did you know that in Florida there exists an outlawed subspecies of human beings? I'm one of these undesirables I've become a misfit, a subhuman, a throw back to the ape when it first became human and started walking upright

I am therefore a threat to our mayor and to civilization because I do not drive an automobile, nor like him, do I have a chauffeured limousine

My mayor is so focused on moving traffic that all the old-fashioned safety rules of lights were eliminated to have four wheels crisscross quickly and to eliminate useless people who still need to, or try to, walk

This is being done to eliminate all undesirables on two legs to make room for more four-wheels and thus not to remind people that they got off all fours to walk upright on their hind legs, and now have come back on all fours, but attached to wheels

We pedestrians (who use only two legs) are bad reminders of the early attempts to stand up In Aventura we are more than expendable, and we need Dr. Kevorkian to help clean up this disturbing vestige- or else we must choose(which we deserve) to be mowed down by this rushing, rushing, crisscrossing traffic

To beautify Aventura for drivers, the mayor cloned Barbie-doll-like trees along the boulevard and placed an expensive metal stand to block right of-way passages for willful, desperate pre humans like me

I also had no idea how much Miami is a parking lot and when I got information about how to go somewhere, I was told that the address is behind a parking lot (but not told about how many parking lots were in front of and behind the ones in front of before the one that was in front of the one I was to find the right parking address

Future Species

For the skin and fur for clothing. The pain and torture of an animal crying, knowing it will be murdered by the smell of death, remains strongly etched in my physiology, in my memory, in my entire self Maybe people will develop plants and trees that do not require human nutrition - to be related to predatory solutions for food

Some species will develop the use of scrap metals and pollutants and other waste products and thus clean up the environment for a new group of species, and thus changing from being a predator of live beings to purifying the previous evolution And the Jews who fit in the category of the chosen will be eliminated by the survival of the meanest

The evil ones consider themselves blameless Since they deny their own badness, they must perceive others as bad They project their own evil onto the world they see it in others

A Solution For Our President

How our President can change the problem of diversity in Democracy (financial, political, religious and social differences), which he told us he wants to do

Since Adam and Eve lost their heavenly childhood in the Garden of Eden by eating the fruit of the matured tree of knowledge, which resulted in their becoming aware of sex and that they have to labor to get their food, we, their descendants have become compulsive about both food and about sex The greatest of evolutionary change from plant life resulted in the problems of today.

Animals depend both on animal and plant life for survival, while plant life depends only on the sun, the rain and the soil for survival This evolutionary change in food is the root of all present evil If that need would be eliminated, all our problems would disappear again.

If only Adam and Eve would not have made that terrible mistake of eating that particular fruit of knowledge, or perhaps better still, not eaten at all? This eating progressed to our eating meat, which started with the need to kill in order to get the meat, and then developed many new ways to kill Once we learned how to kill, then wars became easy and necessary

If we didn't want such food, there would be no poverty and no need for politics and politicians, and certainly no little Red Riding Hoods with bad wolves to frighten little children about being eaten

If people would simply return to living again like plants, using the sun and rain, and with their feet firmly in the soil, there would be no need for guns and its amendments, no need to have class discriminations, no need for political parties to raise so much money, and no need for taxes to support them

By eliminating the desire for present kinds of food, it would also eliminate sex with rape, abortions, kidnapping of children, and jealousy murders And of course present diseases with so many medical expenses So simple to solve - if we, like plants would only return to our dependence on the sun, the rain, and the soil for our survival, we could be back in the Garden of Eden at once

Quotes

Degree Of Maturity

Judaism expects and demands a greater maturity than many people are ready to accept It is much easier to reject this degree of maturity by hating the Jews for it The difference in responsibility is so much greater and stronger that the result even causes many Jews to hate Jews

Life

Life is full of mistakes, misunderstandings and misinformation

Islam

When a young child is disappointed in its mother, the child must not show too much anger towards her, (for survival reasons), so it turns it's anger towards her sister instead, perhaps just like Islam people who are unhappy, (perhaps with it's government or religion), their rage is turned against others

The Art Of Being Human

Learn how to lie Do everything to hurt others Wear lipstick to cover your unclean thoughts and words Blame someone else for your wrongs

What Is True

What is true can be partially false, and what is false can be partially true

Statements

A statement that means actually what is said, can mean the opposite to some people (form of projection), it is what the person wants it to mean

Stealing

Stealing people's money is called taxes Forcing strangers to take care of your children and support them for you is called poverty.

Formal Letters

The letters that follow, both formal and personal are important to the Author to include in this book They express her feelings during certain periods and events in her life You will understand after you have read the letters

Sheik Wagdi Ghonieon – New York Post

Dear Sheik Wagdi Ghonieon,

I was not aware that I am a descendant of the apes until you informed me And I am most grateful to you for this information because until now I never understood why you hate me so At last I understand! I like apes even though I didn't know that I was related to them

I really like them better than some people

Sincerely, Not

Mr Thomas Sobol - State Education Department

Dear Mr Sobol,

I understand you are heading a project, which I am

totally interested in, and I would like to offer my help, salary free

I am particularly interested in the minority problem, as I have been studying this for twenty years I would like to know how many minority types are to be studied and which minorities are going to be included and which are going to be excluded

I am a clinical psychologist (not a historian) and I am offering my help free, under your guidance Sincerely yours,

Mr Crouch - Daily News

Ref. your August Article

Dear Mr Crouch,

It is interesting that you mention one single country that is receiving money from U.S You forgot to mention how much Arafat gets, how much Egypt gets, and the others

If our politicians weren't giving so much to the others, then Israel would not need to accept anything to defend itself and Democracy

Sincerely, A Devoted Reader

Woody Allen

Dear Woody,

I love your loudly - heard evaluation of Israel!

I think you are so right, and I hope you will prove it to the world by going there yourself and standing right between the innocent Palestinians and the wicked Israelis, to demonstrate your even- handedness

In this way you can instantly become the New-World Messiah, and save the world

Sincerely yours,

Mr Dershowitz – Warner Book

Dear Mr Dershowitz,

I am particularly interested in the concept of justice, and therefore found your book "Just Revenge" as most important

I was, however, disappointed in its ending Your ending would be very pleasing to readers in general, but it is not based on reality There is just too much evidence that genetic inheritance is not meaningless There can be exceptions where the line of inheritance is stronger or weaker from one source, but it is not eradicated that easily

I do wonder how you would have ended it if you had not dismissed that fact?

Sincerely yours,

Kathy Sprague – Town Assessor

Dear Town Assessor,

Instead of protecting us, we were forced by threats to remove our lifetime home buildings in order to protect our neighbor below us from hurting himself when he kept breaking in our buildings to steal our belongings

Now that taxes still keep increasing, even under such circumstances, can you please tell us how much I am paying extra for the people who call themselves a new "religion" in order not to pay their taxes?

And why have these neighbors been allowed to have their electric poles on our property without our permission?

Sincerely yours,

County Division of Planning – Gov Center

Dear Sirs,

I have not answered you any sooner because of my pained feelings regarding what were our lifetime homes

I was forced, by those who give themselves the power, by threats, to remove our buildings This was in order to protect the neighbor below us and others from injuring themselves when they would break in to steal our possessions

I find it hard to understand why the punishment is for the victim instead of the victimizer Perhaps you could explain this to me

Sincerely yours,

Laurie Dutcher - Tax Collector

Dear Ms Dutcher,

I am enclosing one check for the three separate bills for school taxes. You have been very kind in responding to me before, and I would so appreciate if you would provide me with some additional information, such as the amount or percentage of my taxes that I am paying for those who do not pay taxes. Perhaps I can feel good knowing the amount of charity I am providing for others

You are most unusual in answering me before and I truly appreciate and honor you for this

Sincerely yours,

Mr Clifton - Executive Editor Miami Herald

Ref "The Neighbors" April 1999 "Families Of severely disabled face dilemma over what to give up" by Mireidy Fernandez

Dear Mr Clifton,

The D'Angelos's 25-year old son who is severely disabled, has a day companion and receives 96 diapers each month, but uses six diapers a day To toilet train him, they had a therapist for six months, and the family had to give that up in favor of more diapers

I would like to recommend a solution for you to give to his constitutionally creative lawyer Why not have the toilet training therapist spend even a small part of those six months and teach the loving parents, as well as the companion, how to toilet train the son, and even teach the Aunt and Grandparents who all love him?

P S Enclosing copies of your article with pictures

Sincerely, Not

Mr Metcalf - Lighthouse for the Blind

Dear Mr Metcalf,

You will never be forgotten by so many of us In this way, you have already attained immortality!

All our love and best wishes, Not Famous

Mr Alan Nichols – President - Lighthouse for the Blind

Dear Mr Nicholas,

As a current and long-time member of the Lighthouse for the Blind, I feel the need to involve you as their volunteer President of the Board in a situation that involves an ex-employee, Mr Larry Lawhorn

It seems that I am the so-called chosen person who does not worry about stating an opinion that is shared by many, and thus, I am taking this opportunity to do just that

I have the good fortune, or perhaps the misfortune, of being privy to a hearing whispered comments from many of the participants expressing their sadness about the loss of Larry Lawhorn and the way he was dismissed. You need to know that people are not happy The joy we have experienced during our time there with the previous administration, made the Lighthouse a very special place for the clients to feel wanted and cared for

Larry was responsible for those feelings. He is an integral part of creating an atmosphere conducive to the needs of the clients and sometimes beyond their needs It has turned into a pervasively saddened environment without him there to lend a helping hand and good work. Certain somberness has replaced the contented climate that existed prior to his departure.

We are all feeling devastated and emptiness for losing Larry We admired him tremendously for his accomplishments for the Lighthouse He worked seven days a week and long hours He did the networking for the entire Lighthouse and on his own time He volunteered numerous extra hours and even paid for many extras to save the Lighthouse many thousands of dollars

The staff, clients, and volunteers are all distraught by such a great loss It is not easy to maintain a devoted and committed employee, and we feel that the new Director should have more carefully made her decision and perhaps asked the long-time clients for input before making such a destructive decision

On behalf of many of us, please consider bringing Larry Lawhorn back to his previous position at the Lighthouse, where he is much needed and sadly missed

Sincerely yours,

Joyce Brothers - New York Post

Dear Joyce Brothers,

In your column of May 11th in the 'New York Post' referring to the book "Confronting Crime" by Elliot Currie, with which you say you agree, you say inequality of wealth leads to crime

I would appreciate it if you would clarify this by answering these questions

1. When in our history did we have greater equality?
2. Do you feel that you yourself commit no crimes only because you are not in want?
3. Why is it that so many people who are in want do not commit any crimes?

I would appreciate your comments I am enclosing a self addressed stamped envelope for a personal reply

Sincerely yours,

President George W Bush – The White House, Washington, D C

Dear President Bush,

I have no reason to defend anyone except for the obvious purpose of justice or fairness And since you appear to be really working for justice, which is rare in people of great power, I would like to bring to your attention for examination and correction, without prejudice, which appears to be a lack of justice in relation to the treatment of Pollard vs Robert Hanssen I am referring to a documentary shown February 18, 2002 on T V channel A&E about Robert Hanssen, the worst American spy, who was responsible, not only for twenty years of treason, murder of American FBI agents, and other untold harm, he is given even the rights to keep his pension, his home, etc, and is treated with compassion and respect for being a religious man

In the case of Pollard, he not only never even gave information to an enemy country, but gave information to Israel that had not only been promised to them, but was a promise not being kept, even when it was a serious danger to them from Iraq

I realize that it is part of human nature that most people seek scapegoats in order to make themselves feel and look better But this never really helps them at all and only creates more injustices in the future, for themselves, as well as for others

I do not know if you, or anyone else will even read this, but I hope I am mistaken about that, and that somehow I might be informed that you at least heard me This matter seems to have some similarities to the Dreyfus Affair P.S I am enclosing corroborating data

Respectfully yours, Not

President Bill Clinton - The White House

Dear President Clinton,

You told us that you do not know what "is" is

Personally I find what "is" just is No matter how I define it. For instance, when death occurs, whether I define it as going to heaven, or being reincarnated, or any of the other definitions - no matter what I call it, or describe it as - I find that it always means that it is And I have to accept what is, no matter how I try to fool myself.

I find it difficult to even fool others, though I say "He is still here with me" I do wish you would tell me how I too could make what is to not be, the way you can

Sincerely, Not

Note I received an answer from President Bill Clinton His answer to me was "he was not going to answer my letter"

National Tax Payers Union

Dear Hopefuls,

Please tell me how you imagine you can possibly accomplish getting the fair tax passed considering the massive I R S

Federal employees who profit from this unfair mess and would not give it up, nor the endless accountants and lawyers and all their relatives, friends, and their attachments? If you could do this, I would certainly love to help in every way

Sincerely yours,

Personal Letters

Mr Herbert Solon

Dear Mr Solon,

I keep calling you endlessly and when I do reach you on the phone, you keep repeating that you are taking care of my case against Mr Sullivan, and you and another lawyer have been working on it, and you keep reminding me that you have paid $60 for serving papers on him and his nephew in October 1972 (to get him to return my money which you had advised and arranged for me to give him in the first place) You took all my papers then (and you knew I had no copies) and all this time you have been reassuring me over and over that you completed the necessary steps, and that they were served and the SEC was notified and you assured me of success

You repeatedly told me this on the telephone as well as the times you permitted me to come to your office You said I would receive corroboration in the mail from you and your other lawyer When I later reminded you that I had not, and that I still didn't know his name, and couldn't you give me his telephone number so I could call him? I asked you for something in writing since I had been waiting for over a year You became defensive and accused me of not trusting you Then, for the first time, you actually said that neither of the men had been served because you didn't believe the nephew was legally responsible (although you were the one who had decided he was) Until now you repeatedly told me that both were responsible and that he was actually served and that the SEC was holding him responsible for causing me to have had to hire another lawyer to get back my money from Mr. Dana to whom you had me pay $2,500 as a retainer fee. Mr Dana also kept telling me for years that everything was being done but that it takes a great deal of time to get on the calendar, and other fantastic lies It was only by accident that I learned that I was being deceived by him It was my dentist whose brother, also a lawyer, had overheard something about what was being done to me, and my dentist told me. (Of course to get my money back by another lawyer – although it was almost instantly – I had to pay an even higher fee)

All these years I never suspected it was you who had my money all those years which you had Mr. Dana pretend that he was the one, and of course my having paid it to him And all those years I never suspected it could be your fault and you kept making me believe it was the fault of Mr Dana! It was only after your remark that I finally suspected and realized that the money returned to me through hiring a third lawyer, which had been possessed by you for years – and the matter completely and forever neglected – and yet you continued your endless lies over endless telephone calls! All this time this money was yours through Mr Dana, and that Mr Dana was merely the person who took the money for you

When I finally realized all the cruel harm you did and the years of hanging me in the air to toss slowly in the air, the thousands of telephone calls and the numerous trips to your office you requested from me – my hurt was so great that I could only respond impotently and therefore unable to do anything. I have been turning my other cheek for so long This and you are the last straw You always claimed to be our friend and we trusted and believed you, and you betrayed our every trust and your every word

Even the money you took for filing a mortgage (You insisted on receiving it in cash but finally agreed to accept part of it by check) Always repeating that you were picking up the mortgage papers for me – and you would keep asking me to call you back endless times, and each time you begged me to wait because you were picking it up that day, the next, and whatever excuse you could make – or someone else was picking it up for you – or had picked it – and always telling me that it was definitely filed You would imply that I didn't trust you and you would get angry You even told me that you had picked it up and your papers were somewhere or other, and therefore I couldn't pick it up myself

And what about all the matters you supposedly did for my husband, and then you always kept what you were supposed to forward to him? I can't imagine what you did with the other people I recommended to you.

And what about the most serious matter of all which involved my sister and her daughter, whose husband Steven Bland was responsible for her being in a coma You assured us that he and his wealthy family would pay the hospital bills, - and your concern and promises! Until all the witnesses disappeared (we were told the witnesses had been paid off) – and so much later when you returned some of my papers, and there, to our extreme surprise, I found the medical bills that had never even been submitted, but had been paid by my husband

It never occurred to us that the man of the legal profession would be lying to his client again and again, and on such matters In retrospect, I can't imagine how I could have been so deceived I am still the innocent farm girl and stupidly trusting lamb that believed that all people have the integrity and morality that my very poor and completely uneducated farm parents instilled in me

The injuries and intellectual rape you have imprinted upon me are beyond imagination – and in a civilization run by your profession – is far greater than all the monetary losses you were responsible for on our behalf

Sincerely, Not

Mr Oscar J Cohen - Letter 1

Dear Mr Cohen,

I received your letter with Mr Solon's statement and did not answer sooner because I felt so outraged As you yourself can easily see Since Mr Solon lied to me about everything while I was his client, it is only natural that he would do no differently for himself.

I am enclosing a copy of the letter I wrote to him on August 1973 from which you can get a picture of some of the things that I know about and have proof I am enclosing some of the details relating to the matters brought up.

It took me a long time to realize that Mr Solon is a psychopathic liar, for he appears so kindly and I really thought so well of him

Mr Oscar J Cohen –Letter 2

Dear Mr Cohen,

I will try to explain what happened on September 7th. Judge Schwartz assigned me to Judge Wolm. I waited in the room where Judge Wolin was to preside

I noticed that Mr Solon and Roth were busily coming and going repeatedly After a while Mr Roth (Mr Solon's attorney) came over to me and said I was to follow him to another room I trustingly followed him and it was not until much later that I realized that I was led to a different judge, arranged by Mr Roth How else? The judge Mr Roth took me to was judge Sclar, who at first pretended as if he was helping me because he said to Mr Solon and Mr Roth that I needed help because I was undefended Very soon, I realized I was mistakenly naive when none of my evidence was even looked at and instead

Judge Sclar just looked down and said to Mr Roth that all this is proof against myself

I couldn't believe that it was possible for even the worst kind of human being to do and say such a thing and I immediately felt paralyzed by the hopelessness of it all Then Mr. Roth, with a great act of Hollywood showmanship, said to me "Where did you get that manila envelope?" I didn't know what he was referring to and pointed to everything I had for him to show me He pointed to a folded piece of paper on which I had written some notes and dates about the Geico matter, and accused me of having stolen my papers from Mr Solon's office! I expected the judge to inquire about this but he had no intention to do so I felt so hurt and by such a fantastical extreme trumped up lie, and realizing the judge was set up for this, that after hearing Mr Solon's lies to questions asked him by the step-up-judge, so that when the judge asked me if I had any questions to ask Mr Solon, I knew it was all useless, and all I could say was "You will all have to sleep with yourselves while remembering what you have done to me Judge Sclar dismissed the case

I spoke to Mr Friel, assistant district attorney, who advised me to inform you, the bar association and to go to Criminal Court about Mr Solon's remark about having a bullet put through my head and about Mr Roth accusing me of stealing my papers

My problem is that I am afraid that Mr Solon who claimed to be friendly with some Mafia clients will carry out his threat

Mazel Davis

Dear Mr. Davis,

American Savings Bank of Florida has informed me that you have not received my savings book which Gary, manager, has mailed to you because the US post office refuses to deliver your mail when addressed to

East Savings Bank in the City.

And that you request a ten dollar fine from me instead of fining the post office for keeping the mail, instead of, at least, returning it to the sender

Now since I don't want another book, and don't need another book for transferring my account, I would like to have an explanation from you that has an iota of rationality to it

I realize the educators today do not believe in logic, and that logic may not return for at least one or two generations from now, but even if you want to make everything relevant to nothing, I absolutely can not pay for something I don't want and don't need

So perhaps you can mail some forms for me to sign so that I can withdraw at least part of my money until you bravely contact your post office

I am enclosing a copy of my receipt from the Am Savings Bank sent to you about two months ago with my book, etc – which has my account and amount of balance (before interest and direct deposits)

New School for Social Research

Gentlemen,

I wish to thank you for refusing me re-admission to your school You have thus spared me from further years of fruitless and non-educational "education" in your school.

It was the persistent suggestions of someone in your school that I re-applied for admission This was in opposition to all my feelings because of the irrationality, which many others and I have experienced from your previous faculty and past heads of the school And at this person's insistence and reassurance of the improvement of your school heads and faculty, I again asked for admission.

Now even you consider the previous administration as adequate judges in grading me poorly, and yet, at the same time, you consider them inadequate in admitting me as a PhD student

This in itself shows me that the irrationality of the school is continuing in the new administration, and such a school cannot deserve my respect Thank you for not accepting me

Sincerely yours,

Jean - Friend

Dear Jean,

I addressed the envelope to you a long time ago but I am finally writing to you today Partly because I get so involved in doing nothing that I forget about the passing of time But mostly it is that I am so stressed trying to do things, and avoiding doing them, and being frustrated because of it

And it is very hard for me to talk to someone when there is no response - E-mail helps that to some extent because it is so fast I had a copy of the New York Post yesterday and it has so much more of what I know and am interested in than the local papers - but I hate to pay so much for it down here I miss so much of the news by not seeing it In some ways, it is like living in a different country Perhaps you can fill me in on with some of it Looking forward to hearing from you.

PS I am enclosing the article about Hillary that I told you about

Jenny - Niece

Dear Jenny,

I'm not sure I know what you want to know It would be mainly lab work and usually you get information in different instructors and find out different areas of study that particularly interest you and which is available to you You have to start somewhere, do you want to be there before you begin?

Your father said you are dissatisfied with the school and that you are lonely Everyone is lonely when they start somewhere new What do you expect? The school sounded so wonderful to me. I don't know what the instructors are like, but there must be some that are good

Do you feel you are not appreciated enough? It is not their purpose to replace parents and friends If you spend your time really studying hard, you will not be lonely much longer I promise you that. Let me know what you think your problems are.

Love, Your aunt

Sadye - Friend

Dear Sadye,

Since I have no idea of who or what was said to whom, I feel it is necessary for me to disappear so as not to upset you so Your resentment toward me goes way back from the beginning of time, and I do not know how to alleviate it

I do feel saddened by this, but I just have too much to bear without adding this, whatever it is I have really tried hard to help all the ways I know how Even Shirley-the-Great said to me reproachfully "Why don't you let Philip buy the place? Does Shirley really believe that I have been stopping him? Is that what you believe?

When I told her that Philip has been saying this for months but so far he hasn't I said to her "I'm not sure how reliable he is because he is disturbed. Shirley answered me angrily "I don't find him disturbed at all" I said. "All right, if he is not disturbed, then it is I who am disturbed It is what she believes and it is apparently what you believe And so it is and what else can I say?

Sondra - Friend

Dear Sondra,

Misunderstandings occur very easily I am un-aware of what terrible things I must have said, or if someone else misstated it for me I apologize for whatever I said or didn't say. I do sometimes make satiric remarks, which not everyone understands unless they know me well

How many Hail Mary's would get your forgiveness? Or what atonement is acceptable?

Marcia Bennett-Bernier – Friend - Letter 1

Dear Marcia,

I am so sorry to hear about your father I feel especially pained about it, and for you, because I have had these experiences and more

Most of this is caused by, or aggravated by, the new definition of democracy that all people are equal, whether competent or not, conscientious or uncaring, good or evil Many deaths can be attributed to this notion of equality

I hope things are better for you Let me know, if I can be of help in any way

Love,

When you get a chance, please send me the list that you said you would, of all my additional items that you took – and the prices – so I can have a matching list – before we forget

Marcia Bennett-Bernier – Friend - Letter 2

Dear Marcia,

Today is my birthday, and it is over 6 months since I wrote to you, and I haven't heard from you at all I hope nothing too troubling has kept you from doing so

As for me – I would have written sooner again but I have had, and still have a disturbing family problem that has been making me crazy, (I've been defrauded of all my assets by a relative, and I don't want to hurt the rest of the family.)

I hope you have better news Please let me know what has been happening I hope, especially, that you feel real well

Regards to Alex, I do wish we could have a real long talk Remember that you are always welcome where I am

Love,

Marcia Bennett-Bernier – Friend - Letter 3

Dear Marcia,

I can't tell you how disappointed and hurt I was that you would not return my calls when I was in New York I thought you would be pleased to return my unsold things

I am therefore forced to consider reporting the loss of my merchandise but to be sure I do not incorrectly report what you sold and owe me for, and the things you admit you still have, please send me this information now so I can check off from my lists

I hope you are well and much happier
Love,

Marcia Bennett-Bernier – Friend - Letter 4

Dear Marcia,

I keep waiting for you to keep your promises, and I am more disappointed than ever The things that you have admitted to having sold, you still haven't paid me for And you have not returned any of my most valuable items. For instance, whatever you returned I marked off and you only returned some of the paintings but none of the valuable ones And that applies to everything that you even bothered to return

When I speak with someone on the phone. I usually take notes So when you told me you stopped using my electric bed and folded it up to take up less space, I told you that you could sell it so I could get only $500 And you could keep the rest And you agreed This bed has a special motor, which never needs repairs of any kind, and this bed is not replaceable

Then when I had a customer for it for you, you suddenly told me that you don't know what happened to it What would you think if I talked to you like that?

The same thing about the huge quartz – Maybe someone stole it This quartz was so big and heavy that even the strongest man could not go off with it And it was a most unusual and beautiful specimen

All the small and very desirable collectable items, you seem to have lost all records of and all memory of, so you ask me to send you the list and now you have remained silent since you saw the copies in your own handwriting. What do you expect me to do? I have always, not only liked you very much, but also trusted your honesty, and I was always concerned for your welfare

I wish you were capable of being more truthful with me If you wish to pay me for the things you admit to have sold, then I will not include them in the police report

NOT FAMOUS

(P s Your boyfriend Alex accidentally admitted to me that he had the bed)

My best wishes,

Marcia Bennett-Bernier – Friend - Letter 5

Dear Marcia,

I still feel sorry for you - knowing that you will have to keep lying to yourself for the rest of your life -to cover your guilt -for stealing all my valued possessions (mine and my parents) knowing bow desperate I was to have to leave everything with you, who pretended to be a friend who could be trusted - all in the hope of saving my hopelessly dying husband

Perhaps you can send me a copy of your dreams?

Marcia Bennett-Bernier – Friend - Letter 6

Dear Marcia,

Your mouth kept going, going, going very fast like a guilty war machine. Never stopping from spewing out your factory of lies

I used to defend you and I used to think you were capable of being a friend, and I couldn't help myself but feel sorrow for what I once thought of as a human being and as a friend

I always felt kindly toward you, and I couldn't help but feel sorry for you that you should need to prostitute yourself by perjuring yourself in order to steal everything from my family and me

In Memory of you,

336

Olga - Friend

Dear Olga,

You are poisoning yourself with your thoughts. Instead of thinking of how you can solve each problem, you think how someone is at fault in not doing it for you

You keep reminding yourself constantly what and how someone else did it wrong, and especially how someone did it wrong only to you and against you

This is the way you are poisoning yourself and it is the way to drive yourself mad, and that is the way mad becomes crazy

You get mad when someone else doesn't know, or do, everything, but you don't think you are supposed to do or know everything You forget that everyone is as human as you are

You get mad when, something is not immediate for you, but no cure is immediate except death

You get mad_____

You get mad_____

You get mad_____

You get mad_____

You can list all the things you are mad about, including me and everyone and everything, and then let us talk about it

Love,

Sally - Friend

Dear Sally,

At last I see why lawyers are unable to help me with a justice trust! It is because lawyers are taught not to understand what justice means

For example, lawyer President Clinton, a Rhodes and Oxford scholar, admitted he doesn't even know what "is" is He suffered such pain from this lack of knowledge that he admitted it before the entire world

Mr Jacobowitz sent you the information for which he had charged me $648 80 The information was still secret from me, only the charges were not secret. Is this a lawyer's way of thinking? And now you feel it only right that I be expected to pay again for the same information now given to you?

You helped lawyer Saul Feder steal $2,500 from me by generously feeding him unbelievable misinformation, which his criminal mind, found very useful Of course, it was not intentional on your part, but does a lawyer's justice mean that I should pay for others' mistakes as well as my own? Is this the meaning of justice?

Sincerely, with love,

To The Town

Madam/Sir,

American Indians had owned our property, that our parent's purchased unseen because they couldn't afford more

People came to get water on the property and called it "Long Leban Vaser".

There was (and is) their burial grounds, which my mother did not permit me to dig up, which I wanted to do so much There is a cave up on the hill where there are Indian drawings and objects on the walls

And now, the amount being used for those you do not pay taxes added on to the amount I was forced to pay with the threat of confiscation of my property and forced to remove all our life-long family buildings in order to protect a neighbor who kept breaking in to steal our stoves, refrigerators and antique furniture and belongings, to protect him in case he got hurt while doing this

Sincerely, Not Famous

Personal Stories

Mother Hen

She called herself the mother hen She decided what is her table, her house

She felt good about this and was very proud and wanted everybody to know how good she was because she was the mother hen

She chose everything first for herself and her decisions were the only correct ones, correct for everyone of course

Yes, everything had to be her way and if anything was not so, the other person had to be very guilty

She watched her table for a chick to disobey and that chick got a barrage of accusations added to the actual one.

Yes, she was a real mother hen the same way I experienced it on the farm.

The mother hen would take the baby chicks under her wings, but when a chick was injured, the mother hen would peck at the injured chick until the chick was dead

As a small child my mother would have me take care of an injured chick to keep it away from its mother until the injury was healed before it could be safely returned to its mother hen.

This human mother hen said to the injured chick (that's me) "You can't sit at my table anymore"

This chick felt it was her own fault for not having left earlier She said to mother hen "Ok" but wanted to also say "Thank you for freeing me from your control, and giving me back my freedom"

So you can now see the similarity of this mother hen and the nature of mother hens

The Cricket Guest

I didn't know that crickets came with smoke detectors My live-in cricket actually came later, but I'll never know when, because they both seemed to have the exact same pitch and both usually made these short chirp-like sounds

Before I discovered I had the cricket as a guest in my home, I used to wonder why the smoke detector went off while I was sleeping I would get out of bed and check the stove and hallway for fire

I knew that it lived with me, I couldn't always tell, though for the last two or more months, my cricket felt safe enough to chirp almost constantly

It stayed within the vicinity of the smoke detector but sometimes traveled to other areas I had never seen him but must have come close to touching him when I heard him moving on my desk, as I was about to turn on a lamp there In fact, he sounded only inches away as I was typing

It was not until I actually saw one near my lamp that made me really sure of his existence At times he seemed to chirp almost constantly Though I was glad he was there I actually feared touching him or even seeing him in this inappropriate environment – knowing what crickets look like Before seeing it, I sometimes heard movements on my desk, and it would scare me. They looked like dried skeletons on tall straw legs I was also afraid I might kill it by mistake since they were hardly seeable and didn't seem to have any body at all

Several people, who heard him and discovered his identity, asked me what I feed him While I was surprised by this question, I wondered if I was starving him I opened the terrace door often enough to free him if he needed to, or wanted to leave, but it seemed he wanted to be out of the cold

While we only saw one, for all I know, the cricket may not have been alone, because they would not be recognizable to me when not together Perhaps when there was constant chirping, it was his conversation with others present or elsewhere, and they may even be hatching a slew of themselves, for that is probably what crickets do

Later on, the cricket had been singing beautiful songs at times, perhaps in anticipation of spring mating When later I couldn't hear him at all and was concerned that his lifespan was up, I felt it as a loss

However, one night I heard him cheerfully chirp away and it brightened up everything again for me

But President Reagan's wife, according to a newspaper article, had a similar visitor in the White House, and she felt afraid too, as I did, but she said that she had arranged for its removal

What do you think was strange about this? That a cricket landed in a city apartment on the seventh floor and was competing with smoke detector?

Not to me What was unbelievable to me was that I could feel guilty about a cricket, and that I felt deserted when I thought it was gone

A Soul Sings Inside

About my cricket, it still lived with me later on People I knew did not understand why I did not want to eliminate its existence - just the way our First Lady did at the White House

They see my appreciation of a cricket as something wrong with me Like I was so lonely that I needed a cricket It was not that I didn't know loneliness but more that the people I knew did not understand me

One day a man who was doing some repairs in my apartment heard the cricket and he did understand somewhat He said to me. "It is like having the country inside the city"

Yes it was, but it was also more than that - yes, related to nature and the country - it was that a little ugly bug that could sing like that - for me it had a little bit of whatever God might be, in it

One day last fall as I walked along with a neighbor Anne I picked up one of the colorful leaves

She said to me kindly "What do you need it for? What

are you going to do with it?" I said "I'm not going to do anything with it. It's just so beautiful"

But to her it was a kind of garbage picking

Unconditional Love - Found At Last

Marilyn said to me "I have finally found unconditional love."

She said: "Isn't it a fact that roaches run away from people? That's what it used to be with me"

"But lately they come to me They come from out of hiding and run right into my arms"

Even as I waited on line at the supermarket, a girl next to her watched as a cockroach on the counter, ran toward her and onto her arm

The cashier too said she never saw anything like that before. The cashier, though pleasantly surprised, helped the customer reject this loving gesture

Thus Marylyn has finally discovered true unconditional love, if not by a man, then by a man's ancestor

A Summer Day In Manhattan

The weather was so cheerful that it made Ruth feel better as she walked briskly toward the station She was pleased with herself for getting up while everyone else was still asleep But at the same time, she felt sorry for herself, because she, too, might have slept late, as it was Thanksgiving Day

It would take her at least four hours to travel back and forth from Croton to New York City and pick up her altered dress but it was that important Even her dressmaker had opened especially for her

Ruth couldn't bear to let Hubert see her again in anything she had worn before Her fiancé felt displeased enough with her, as it was This was a black, sleek, sophisticated dress that revealed her to advantage, the kind Hubert always admired on other girls This dress, she thought, might help her start all over again with him on their Thanksgiving date

Settling herself on the empty train, Ruth felt lonely Except for some railroad men, everyone seemed to be staying home today She let her mind drift back to the subject that obsessed her these days As she thought of the way Hubert sometimes looked at her, it made her collapse within herself and she sank lower into her seat Even worse were the times when he would look at her, yet not see her at all Painfully, she remembered everything in detail that she had worn for him and all the different ways she had tried to look to please him Disappointments were associated in her mind with everything she wore

Ruth found the same deserted loneliness in the city, on the subway, and on the streets She was satisfied, however, that she had come, for her trip was successful She left the little shop hugging her package to her, feeling secure and confident Hubert couldn't help but notice her in this new dress She pictured him with his eyes sparkling as they used to when he told her endearing things

She was beautiful and brilliant when he used to think

so But now that he noticed everything wrong with her, she couldn't help but do everything wrong Somehow she couldn't carry herself the way she used to Parts of her body just didn't work together

She often spoke the opposite of what she intended to say Her thinking was not clear, and she could hardly control her emotions when she meant so much to be pleasant and gay. At times she felt herself cringing, and often she recognized a tinge of begging voice

These emotions seemed foreign to her, for they jumped unbidden into the open out of unknown recesses She did not like herself for having them, and it made her feel all the worse

Ruth got to the subway without having been aware of walking there She was aroused into awareness by the feel of mobs on the street And then she saw them

The streets were filled with people, people who were full of longing for new things and new experiences Most of the people were living through the interests of their children Today was Macy's Thanksgiving Day Parade, and they were taking the excited children out for a happy afternoon.

Children were everywhere Parents held some in their arms and others by the hand Every child had a balloon as part of the celebration All the balloons were alike, except that some were blue and some red All were attached to long sharp sticks

Trainmen guarded the outer entrance of the subway station to keep everyone out The trains could not accommodate the crowds The unusual influx of people was met with an even greater scarcity of trains due to the current fuel strike

Ruth waited for thirty minutes in the tightly packed crowd at the 72nd street subway entrance Squashed and squirming frustrated children only heightened Ruth's tense anxiety to get home. Balloons moved unexpectedly toward her from every direction

At last a train was arriving and the doors opened! She shoved her way through, thinking only of getting back to Hubert. Clutching her token desperately, she finally got near a turnstile only to hear a guard shouting: "No downtown trains! Only uptown trains at this station today"

Frantically she pushed her way out and tried to hail a taxi. Time was passing! No empty taxis! The bus, packed to bursting, would not stop After twenty minutes of rushing about wildly, she forced her way into a stuffed bus. Children took up extra space as they wriggled about The bus crawled down the avenue

Wrapped up in her own anxiety, Ruth only half heard parents begging their children to keep quiet while they cried for seats and attention

They screamed and jumped for their balloons, as parents tried to hold them up high out of passengers' eyes

Forty-five minutes later, Ruth got to the street, irritable and nervous, but she still had to make her way eastward Empty taxis apparently didn't run on the avenue Precious time was passing!

She had already missed two trains, and if she did not make this one, Hubert surely wouldn't wait At last a cross-town bus stopped But trucks kept getting in the way, as if conspiring to keep her from getting to the station If only there were no traffic lights!

It took people forever to get in and out of the bus The children kept dragging behind with their balloons catching onto everything on the avenue! If only she could get to the avenue, she'd take the shuttle to Grand Central Station. That might save time. The bus just sat and did not move Two minutes! Three minutes! Anything would be better than this standing still The nervousness of the people around her made her even more jittery.

Unable to stand it any longer, Ruth jumped out of the car and raced through the streets, startling the children and upsetting their balloons as she reached the shuttle entrance

Arriving at Grand Central, Ruth found it mobbed with holiday travellers She ran, pushing through them, her hair limp, clothes dragging, and feet swollen. Breathlessly, she forced her way past the conductor, who was already closing the gate

Clutching her package, untied and shabby, she sank into a seat The excitement had been too much for her But her hiccups stopped suddenly when the conductor said, "You have the wrong train The next stop is where you get off"

Ruth couldn't understand her feelings For strangely, she felt relieved It was better this way, for Hubert would never be satisfied

As always she had done the best she could But with him, it would always be considered the wrong thing Feeling free for the first time in four years, she straightened up in her seat, and comfortably and happily gazed out of the window

Like An African Queen

She was very tall and stately Though not young, she moved like an African Queen I watched her walk with admiration as I crossed behind her

She wore a long dress and a draped kerchief on her head She suddenly stopped in front of me, and arranging herself by degrees, she pushed her dress way up with graceful competence, and there, with legs wide apart, her dress well draped, and with no undergarments to restrain her, remaining very gracefully upright and head high, she urinated in the center of the sidewalk, strongly and for a long time

She urinated right in the middle of the wide triangular sidewalk in the midst of crisscross traffic, on Broadway.

Although she exposed herself all the way, she showed no concern or embarrassment For me, dusk and the blackness of her body aided my embarrassed fascination

Then draping her long skirt back in place, she walked on as before, as queenly as could be

Nrogi And The Scapegoat

We were friendly and helpful in our working proximity for several years until he became concerned about political problems in his native Africa

He then kept badgering me about my lack of concern about this I finally asked him if he expected me to go to Africa and fight there for him, while he remained here in the United States?

I purchased a huge button with the word "Scapegoat" across it and wrote my own name on the top and his name, (after the word "for") under it, and wore it for him to see After a while he realized somewhat what he was doing, blaming me for his own anger and guilt

But soon his wife left him after he explained to his maturing daughter that where he came from, it is permissible to have sex with the father

Do Women Talk Too Much?

I was returning from a late evening class and a woman and three men got on the bus. The woman said "A man is beating up a woman and there is no policeman" One of the men had a whistle and he blew it but still there was no sign of a policeman.

She kept on saying "What a shame it is I don't care what she did he has no right to beat her No One before seemed to think it was their business to interfere and they decided that the woman must have done something to deserve it" She kept repeating it over and over again

I was sitting in front of the bus and I said to the driver "Why not stop there and see what is happening?" He agreed to stop and some passengers rushed up to the front of the bus to see

The bus driver honked his horn as he drove closer The crying woman was a big blond, hysterical and unable to defend herself She ran into the street among the moving cars, and finally, when the light turned red, she got into a cab, but with the man running after her The people in the bus screamed for the taxi not to let him in, but of course he couldn't hear and the taxi rode on with both of them inside The man continued to hit the woman

The bus driver gave chase after the taxi and kept honking his horn The woman in our bus said someone should beat him up The bus driver opened his door and the three men ran out

The taxi stopped and the woman ran out with the man after her The three men knocked the man down The bus driver then drove off and the women passengers went back to their seats. This time the woman had not talked too much

Esther – The Internationally Acclaimed Pianist

Esther complained to me that she can't sleep and asked me to come with her to see a play As soon as we sat down in the theatre she was asleep

Before leaving with Esther, my husband asked me what we were seeing "Esther goes there to sleep, I told him, and even if she's awake she never understands it, unless it is music" Esther gets angry if the story doesn't agree with her ideas, and she wants to teach everyone the correct way that she sees it

Esther had told me that she saw the English movie 'The Chariot" which she liked She said the runner thought they didn't want him to run because of their anti-Semitism, but that it was only in his own mind "The writer didn't think so," I told her

When we got to the theatre, I found out that we were to see two musicals, the second one about Mayor Koch

Before the play began, Esther was immediately asleep in her seat She looked very comfortable there, as if it were her natural sleeping position. The first musical did not wake her She slept on to the end of it and through the long intermission

The second musical "How you are doing, Eddie?" started and she was still asleep The screaming did not wake her As the Mayor screamed on the stage, Esther snored, and since she insists on sitting up front, I pressed her arm, she stopped the snores for a while, but she slept on.

The screams across the stage from the balcony did not wake her. The screams of the bag lady did not wake her The screaming across the stage did not wake her Again the screaming from the opposite side of the stage from the top of the balcony did not wake her The screaming back and forth from the back to front and back again did not wake her

At the last screaming from the entire cast Esther raised her head but her eyes remained closed Then her head went down again.

The loud applause did not wake her It was now 3 1/2 hours that she had slept The lights went on and she awoke and said to me: "I slept through the whole thing" "Don't I know it?" I said As we left she said "It's too early to go home I won't be able to sleep so early"

"Where did you get the flowers? Esther asked me They

were particularly beautiful and I had placed them in the kitchen in two places, because it is the place where I spend most of my time when I return from work. "Would you like some? I asked in answer "You couldn't pay me to have flowers in the house," she answered I had some on the piano and it cost me $800 to repair it when the water from the flowers got into the piano"

"You don't have to have them on the piano." "Where should I keep them, in the kitchen like you? That's no place for flowers, the only place to show them off is on the piano I will never have flowers in the house again" she said

In 1920 Esther was eleven years old, and with her father, her pregnant mother, and her two-year old brother left Odessa, Russia, on a freight train

They were permitted to get transportation by claiming they were going to their hometown near the border They were running away, and the thing to do was to get as far away as they could to another country They had to bring with them necessities, including a chamber pot

When they got off at the border they had to walk to the shoreline - which had extremely sharp declines, both up and down They had to hire two husky men to help them

They then had to wait for midnight because the men were in the transport business illegally They would often murder the people to steal all their belongings In this case they took the family, but said they could not take Esther on the first trip and would have to return for her

What happened to her before she finally met with her family she could not easily talk about and would sometimes deny or change her story? But the abandonment and experience was forever marked deeply within her

This she carried with her during all her musical acclaim, and of course it colored all her remarkable abilities and peculiarities - and was beyond reach for her to free herself from it

The family had to flee Russia at the time because all who were considered capitalists were being annihilated - murdered - and, though her father was not considered to be a capitalist, not having any employees, he was next to that because he was involved in exporting or importing

Under these circumstances, one would imagine that Esther would be passionate against Communism, but instead her nostalgia for those years before her traumatic experiences is much stronger

Esther, though fleeing with her family for their lives, from Communism - yet wishes for an American kind of Communism

The Neighbor And Food Stamps

A woman in the neighborhood telephoned to tell me about her inability to walk much because of a fall She went on to say she had trouble doing her shopping "Can't one of your friends in the building help you?" "No, I have trouble getting anyone," she said

Thinking she might be starving, I agreed to help her, though I live more than fifteen blocks away, and hardly know her

She gave me her order consisting of two dozen cans of cat food, which had to be purchased at a particular store at a particular price

Then she described at which other store I was to go for her grapefruits, how many and at what price And at another more distant store for the fish and the number of slices to be cut, etc

Since I had already agreed to do so, I held my displeasure in check Then she told me to first pick up her food stamps

When I asked her how and where could I possibly do that? "Don't you know?" she answered

"No," I said. "You mean you don't get food stamps! Everybody gets food stamps" "Everyone?" I asked "Everyone I know, everyone living around here," she said

Well, I did her shopping the way she specified, but I never learned how to pick up her food stamps.

Sometimes Anybody Can Be Somebody

I tried and tried to turn on my TV but nothing came on

Finally, I called customer service to tell them and they told me that I should ask anybody and anybody would turn it on for me - just anybody - could turn it on

The next morning, I still did not have anybody, so I expressed my desperation to somebody and somebody did send me anybody

This anybody tried everything he could think of, but it still did not work So he suggested that somebody could do what this anybody could not do

Sadly, this anybody was feeling like a nobody, yet he did continue to try, as anybody would and like anybody, he suddenly turned it on Now, he felt that he had suddenly become a somebody and was no longer an anybody

Since then, when he passes me, he greets me with open arms, as if I were responsible for his discovering the somebody within himself and was no longer anybody

Benji, The Mugger

This story about Benji the mugger occurred in 1991 in New York City before Giuliani became mayor and took responsibility to make the city safe

Benji, and what made the reporter cry!

A NYC newspaper stated that their reporter and photographer had spent six months putting a human face on the fear that grips all New Yorkers and that they had immersed themselves in the world of a street mugger who preys on the people of the city

The first of 4 installments was on June 25, and the last one on July 3, 1991

This very courageous young female reporter was looking for family members of people killed by stray bullets, hoping for an entree into the neighborhood

Her interest in this study was due to her experience

"About two years ago I was nearly carved up in an elevator by a crack addict with a knife It was 8 30p m He dragged me into the elevator at knifepoint I was able to talk him out of stabbing me I moved, and I haven't taken the subway since

"I thought a story on who is committing the runaway street crimes plaguing the city was important enough to take the risks I also knew it had to be done from inside the world of a street mugger - not from the outside looking in

"It wasn't hard finding Benji It was so easy- it was scary It took three random phone calls to the area On the first two calls, there was no answer. Benji's sister Maria answered the third call She said her uncle was shot dead by a stray bullet the previous month

"We spent six months getting to know Benji and his family- sleeping in their streets, meeting their friends"

But this is what made her cry!

Before the reporter arranged to stay with this family, she met them in a restaurant

The reporters sympathetic concern about Maria was the fact they "had never dines in a restaurant" until she met with them six months ago She stated. "They opened their menus, and had no idea what they were reading Appetizers on the left, entrees on the right – they didn't know what those words meant I ordered steak all around Then I went to the bathroom and cried

"The sisters dined in several other restaurants with me By the third time, they learned how to order By the fifth, they brought along Benji and proudly showed him what to do

They told me the war zone they live in and about their family, and that their brother Benji was a street mugger Benji is a textbook case of a sociopathic criminal – but he's not unique There are thousands more just like him out there "And I came to know and care about them.

It took about six weeks for Benji to open up to me, having promised not to reveal his last name, or turn him over to the police"

Welfare helps the family stay home, watch TV, and "play"!

"Benji is now 18 years old His family of eleven lives in a six-room apartment They live mostly on welfare Benji has a 19-year-old brother Mario who has not left the apartment in five years although he is not incapacitated He sits in bed and watches T V 16 hours a day Mario, his 24-year-old sister, has three children Hilda, his 43 year old mother, has ten children from five boyfriends"

Power is "fun" for Benji!

Benji told the reporter "I like victimizing people; I like the excitement of it, Id hate having a boring life" Asked if it bothers him to shoot and stab people, Benji said "No, I feed on it When I think on beating people up, it excites me and I want to do it more"

When Benji was four, his father was shot in the chest and stomach That same year Benji was sent to a foster home where he was beaten with whips and sticks When he was 7, his mother took him back and beat him with belts and broomsticks.

He would throw cats off roofs just for fun At age 9, he started mugging, first with a toy gun, for money but mostly for fun His mother was called to school nearly everyday because he would beat up a teacher or a classmate In the second grade he set fire on the school He dropped out of special school in ninth grade but received a GED diploma

Benji is the only "worker" in the family!

On a busy week, Benji mugs as many as 30 people Sometimes he shoots them And sometimes he thinks its justified – like the time he sliced a mans face from ear to ear for pulling out a knife while he was robbing him

He spends his weekly share of mugger money – about $400, plus jewelry, out of at least $2000 that his little group collects He likes to buy expensive sneakers, jeans, gold earrings and chains. He also buys a lot of beer and junk food. He spent $250 for a handgun and bullets

The only household expense he is responsible for is half of the monthly telephone bill, which is around $100 He said "I am sort of a Robin Hood It makes me feel good if I can give to my brothers and sisters

What would a license for the gun do?

Benji said "Carrying a gun is a status symbol, and shooting someone makes you a high person here. He has shot three people and doesn't remember how many he has stabbed. Once he shot a man for bumping into him in the street

He feels invincible when he mugs, and even mugs people in his own neighborhood because he knows they'll never report him, because they would be dead if they did

He was jubilant to hear about Mayor Dinkins' plan to douse some city streetlights to save money He said, "More people gonna be out muggin, and I'm gonna be one of them" Benji has tried to kill himself more than three times He jumped in front of an oncoming car because his girlfriend broke up with him He was put under psychiatric surveillance for a month "Hopefully someday I'll find me a good woman and she'll settle me down"

Justice for all!

One month after he turned 18, he was arrested as an adult for the first time - on two counts of gun possession "My mother ratted me out four days before Christmas" He used to keep a shotgun and a handgun in the house. One morning he had an argument with his mother over $2 and he threatened to shoot her She turned him in He went to court and received three probations for one count of gun possession The other count was dropped Last month he was arrested for holding up a taxi driver He was released the next day and all charges were dropped

Parenting!

On Thursday, June 27, 1991, the night he tried to murder his mother - he had been out drinking and he was hungry, his younger sisters and brothers were watching T V - "Hey ma, I wanna play wit you Let's play fight." His mother Hilda was getting ready to see her boyfriend

A small, tough-looking woman wearing a bathrobe came out of the next room and pulled Benji to his feet. At 18, he's 5-foot-6, 160 pounds and muscular They slapped and pushed and chased each other around the room, laughing and screaming

"OK, OK, enough now," and she went back to her room Benji followed Hilda tapped him on the shoulder and shoved him out "You don't have to f*ing smack me, Benji snapped" Hilda slammed the door and locked it He kicked the door four times before she opened it a crack, and he threw a punch His fist struck a mirror next to his mother's head, sending glass and wood flying across the room He pounded his mother in the face "Benji, stop I'm not gonna play wit you now" But Benji was not playing anymore, for the third time in his life, he was trying to kill his mother

Only this time the reporter was there. Benji punched his mother in the head and chest over and over again She fell down; he stepped on her face "He's killing Mommy!" screamed Hilda's 15-year old daughter Hilda crawled on her belly out of the living room toward her bedroom

He kept pummeling her with his fists "You don't gotta smack me, you gotta respect me" Hilda reached her room and grabbed a pool cue from behind the door "you're my son You respect me," said Hilda

She raised her arms and with all her might cracked the pool cue over Benji's head His scalp split, and blood gushed "(Why didn't the reporter cry then?)

Benji's friend Robby, who had been watching, held Hilda with one hand and ripped the phone out of the wall so no one could call for help

Benji tried to tear the pool cue from his mother, but his sister Tammy jumped in the way, and Benji twisted and broke Tammy's finger Tammy screamed and a crowd in the street called the cops

Hilda slammed Benji's bleeding head with the pool cue hitting him twelve times He fell to the floor, unconscious, "Go upstairs and call an ambulance" Hilda said to Maria

Mother was unable to take her injured daughter to the hospital because she was waiting to see her boyfriend!

"But Benji was only faking and he lunged onto his

mother, knocking her down and smashing her face again
When the cops arrived, Hilda only felt contempt for them
and refused medical attention"

She said "He tried to kill me I had to hit him because
he didn't listen" Benji couldn't be found and she refused to
press charges Later an ambulance arrived to take Tammy to
the hospital, her hand had swollen to the size of a cantaloupe

Less than an hour after he tried to kill her, Benji was
resting his head on his mother's shoulder as she wiped
blood from his wounds "That's good for you," she told him
"Now go to the hospital and get stitches"

But Benji didn't go and Hilda did not go to the hospital
to get Tammy's hand fixed because she was waiting for her
boyfriend to come over. So Tammy and her sister Maria tried
another hospital They returned home after midnight and
Benji was lying on the couch with his girlfriend, watching a
movie about killer frogs (Why didn't the reporter cry then?)

The reporter said "Before this series of reports even
appeared, Benji had been arrested for robbery with a
weapon, car theft, rape, and also again on sexual assault
and robbery"

Benji told the reporter he would deny everything; no
one could convict him on hearsay"

In the end, even this reporter was surprised when the
commissioner actually agreed with Benji!

The reporter stated "If we can better understand why
they do what they do, we can work toward a solution"

Although she cried because they had never dined before
she had taken them to restaurants, this very courageous
reporter did explain what she had learned that Benji comes

from the world of welfare and dependency, without fathers, and ruined families

And from inept politicians, terrified schoolteachers, and a defeated criminal justice system where the most prosperous men sell dope or women, and where jail is a mere puberty rite

Epilogue (June 15, 2002)

These now very yellowed newspaper articles are eleven years old today But we keep reliving such history- and on a wider scale because people continue to look for excuses to deny the reality of right and wrong, allowing evil to grow by covering it up with idealistic beliefs and avoidance of rational responsibility

It is like what made the reporter cry Learning that they had never dined in a restaurant before!

Hillary, Dorothy And Me

Dear Hillary You say that it takes a village to raise a child It sounds beautiful, but I must confess, I am not sure I understand exactly what it means Hillary, were you raised by a village? If not, in what ways did you suffer for it? Did a village help you raise your child?

Does one have to choose a particular village or will any village do? Or does the child choose it and at what age? And can one keep changing the village whenever one chooses? Or does the village get chosen by one or both parents, or by an objective governmental body, appointed by you?

I am sure I would have been better off if I also had the advantage of being raised by a village Perhaps if I describe some of my friends and neighbors, you could tell us what differences we could have expected?

Before doing so, I thought I should try to find your definition in your book "It Takes A Village" which I am now doing, but I find myself even more confused I am hoping that you will clarify it for me

First you mention that you got the idea from an old African proverb and that children will thrive only if their families thrive and if the whole of society cares enough to provide for them But, Hillary, isn't it a fact that society has been surviving and that it is natural, not only for people, but for animals as well?

Or am I mistaken and this is some new concept? Could the old proverb have been referring to the times when and where populations were very sparse and when communication could exist only when they were face-to-face?

You say that children exist in the world as well as in the family, and that others touch their lives. Dear Hillary, you are so right Many years ago I was very impressed with that when I read Robert Browning's epic poem of 1841 "Pippa Passes" where he tells about Pippa who was 13 years old She worked in a factory morning to night every day except for one day off a year

Pippa got up very early to enjoy her one-day off She went about enjoying her full free day experiencing the pleasure of drinking water from a fountain, of the beauty of the early morning, of nature and of being alive As she went about fully enjoying being with herself, she sang her song "Pippa

Passes" Without being aware of it, she was influencing the lives of the people who heard her as she passed by

(Dear Hillary, Is this what you mean? Or can you mean that people today are avoiding being influenced by others and their environment? And if that is so how is it possible to do this?)

I am going to describe to you my friend Dorothy to see how not having a village to help raise her could have, and has, affected her present life

Dorothy is so competitive about proving that she is not feeling well, that if she were to learn that someone is dying, she would immediately try to prove that she, herself, is dying sooner. She believes she is showing concern and sympathy by proving that she is sicker than anyone else because this is the way she can feel for another person

She likes to ask me questions about myself but never wants to hear the answers because she immediately turns it into something about herself

Dorothy has the appearance of being very motherly and grandmotherly, but she is still the child totally concerned about her survival

(Dear Hillary, Could this have been a failure of her village, or was it due to her not having a village?)

The other day, Dorothy called and asked me "What are you doing?" "Nothing" I said (meaning nothing of importance) Even this she had to top with "Well, you're doing more than I"

Dorothy called and said she can't stand being enclosed by walls; she'd like to go out "All right, where do you want to go?" She told me where she doesn't want to go, and that it is too early to eat and it will be too late to get back. Then she asked "Where should we go"? I said, "You decide; I'll go wherever you want" Then she decided "No, I don't want to go today" "Do you want to go tomorrow?" I asked? "Tomorrow is another day, we'll see," she said

The next morning she called and asked if I have change, and to bring it up to her I said "quarters"? "No, I need a dollar, unless you have change from $10 Bring it up because I'll need a dollar to tip the driver" When I came up, she said "I could have given him five and asked for change"

(Dear Hillary, am I taking the place of a village for her? Is it my duty to do so? Does the need for a village never end?)

She insisted I sit with her and she talked about the uselessness of her life - wanting me to prove her wrong, I thought I said "so if you're useless, so what? Lots of people are useless" That ended it for her and it was ok for me to return to what I had been doing

One time I was ten minutes late in meeting her I told her I had an important long-distance call, but cut it as short as possible. "You're always late" she said, very angry

"Always? Are you always on time?" "Yes, I am" she said. "What about all the times I stand here waiting for you?" "Never," she said "You never see me standing and waiting for you?" "No, never" "You mean when I'm standing here you think it is someone else waiting for you?" "Never," she said, still angry

Later when I told her what the telephone conversation was about, her anger stopped She hadn't believed me, each thing has to be proved to her

(Dear Hillary, is this what a village is supposed to do? Be there to absorb the anger and rage?)

Dorothy is always complaining about her health and exaggerating her ailments to me Through time, I have come to realize that she doesn't do this merely because she worries about serious, life-ending results, but because she needs to have her sisters feel that she is suffering

When she calls her relatives, or when they call her, she stays on the phone a very long time telling them how lucky they are not to be alone and sick

For example, when her sister Clara came from California to visit her in Florida, Dorothy told her that several days before her arrival, she tried to go with me to the restaurant close-by and she could hardly walk and that she wheezed and held on to me – when actually we later walked about for rather a long time at her own choosing and she showed no discomfort of any kind. She then turned to me "Tell Clara isn't it true? Wasn't I too sick?"

Clara tried to persuade her to come and live with her, and Dorothy became very angry. I remembered when once Dorothy complained to me about stubbing her toe because her sister called her late and she had to run to the telephone She called me to ask for Band- Aids, and to tell me how much it had bled But it had not bled, and she had her own Band-Aids and said she had to throw mine away because they weren't fresh, and that she has to buy more

Before Clara's arrival, Dorothy had told me that her daughter had called her lawyer Dorothy was angry with this and she called Clara to tell her off, and that she had upset her She told me that Clara cried I asked her if she had called her back "Why should I, to make her feel better? Why should I make her feel better, I tell her how it is"

(Dear Hillary, Can jealousy have something to do with her feelings? Can the village eliminate or reduce it for her?)

Dorothy is very strong but can't bear any discomfort or pain and says she was never sick nor gave her husband any trouble by being sick She told me her husband did everything for her. She says her life was a very happy one and now that she has pains she wants to die. I often heard her talk and weep to her family members to inform them about how sick and helpless she is

They all want her to come and live with them and to take care of her but she says they don't do anything about it the way she wants She cries on the telephone without tears and they tell her how much they love her and want her - but she wants more proof I used to listen to this continuous cry when she spoke to them Recently she asks me to wait in another room Yesterday I met her cousin who lives near-by I told her "Dorothy says you don't call her" The cousin told me that Dorothy was one of five sisters and she was always the difficult one to please

(Dear Hillary, I am so sorry but I simply forgot to ask her about the village!)

I believe that her sisters were more educated and more socially attractive

Dorothy had to find a way of proving her worthiness by making them feel sorry for her and guilty when they didn't Her remaining sister and her nieces and nephews are required to call her frequently or she becomes very angry with them. Unbelievably angry! It is fascinating to observe

When Dorothy was angry with her sister Clara for not being able to go out to dinner because of her severe constipation, Dorothy turned to me and said. "She is the one who is supposed to take care of me and I have to take care of her!"

(Dear Hillary, Is this what happens because she did not get the sympathy and attention which she was supposed to have gotten from the village?)

Re O J Simpson Dorothy said she believed O J did it, but then decided that Nicole was no angel, and that the prosecutor Clark isn't an angel, therefore now she isn't sure anymore about his guilt

When Dorothy gives me advise - telling me to do something "for my own good", but which seems negative to me - I try to understand - and I believe what she is trying to tell me - is to give me the societal negative reactions often experienced in life and which I should expect - as her helpful advice

(Dear Hillary, Does this mean that she wants to represent the village to me? Or is it that she is training me to be her village?)

When Dorothy would ask me about something and I would admit to her that I couldn't remember, she would always say to me "If you can't remember, it is a lie" Finally, I wrote this and read it to her.

"From now on I don't have to remember or worry about anything I don't have to be concerned about my memory and aging, because if I don't remember, it is only a lie anyway If I don't remember to pay my bills, it is because they are lies I don't ever have to send gifts, birthday cards etc because if I forget, they're lies I don't have to remember to keep my promises - not remember my age, my social security number, and of course I never again have to pay taxes Everything I can't remember is a lie

Isn't it just wonderful! All my problems are now solved"

Since reading this to her, she seems to remember not to tell me "If you forget, it's because it is a lie"

Dorothy arrived at a group holiday dinner and said to me "Where do I sit"? I told her we were given the two seats at the head table, next to the speaker. "I don't want to sit there," she said. "Why should I"? I told her "I didn't choose it This is a place of honor You were given this place with me, but you can sit anywhere you like" "Tell them, she said, I don't want to sit here" "Go and sit where you like" After walking around, she came back and said she would sit where I told her After the dinner, she said she would take the flowers I said, "I was told they go to the participants She said. "Maybe they won't take them." "You can have half of mine," I said. "No, I don't want half" she said

Dorothy suffers when she is not sick She needs to prove to others that she is sick and deserves sympathy When she returned after seeing her new doctor, I asked her what he said "What did he say? He said I am very sick" I asked her if he told her that? "He said I am very sick, what else could he say? He gave me a new cream"

When Dorothy meets people whom she hasn't seen for a while, she tells them "I've been very sick" "What is the matter, what happened?" they ask "What can I tell you, I've been very sick" She asked me to put her package into my bag, which was already full with her folding umbrella, etc and her bag was empty

She had been concerned about the blisters on her foot and called her relatives to tell them that she will never walk again and that she has to sit up all night, as well as days, with her feet up and medications, and is unable to go out But it was Thursday, her day to go to the beauty parlor, and she went to have her hair done When she washes even one dish, she puts on rubber gloves to protect her hands and nails

Dorothy needs to chat with her doctors and to be sure they want to see her again She feels that if she doesn't see them often, she will lose them She told me that she goes to her eye doctor every three months, although she knows what he will say because he always says the same thing - that her sight is perfect, but she feels she has to go in order to keep her doctor "This is America," she said, "this is what you have to do to have a doctor."

To prove that she suffers most- when we both had a cold at the same time - she knew I was doing some home remedies, and she had gone to the doctor for tests and medications - she complained afterwards that I got well by doing nothing and that nothing works for her

(Dear Hillary, How would the village help her with this?)

We met Sylvia and she asked Dorothy how she feels Dorothy told her "I'm a sick lady" "What did the doctor say?" "The doctor should drop dead He said it was nothing, but what can I tell you? I am a very sick lady" "What is wrong?" "Everything is wrong, I'm sick," she repeated

After that she went to see another doctor because of discomfort caused by itching I asked her what he said "He said, it's no good, I am very sick" She continued "he said he can find nothing wrong But what can I tell you"? Dorothy then said perhaps she would need an operation "Do you want an operation?" I asked

I believe that as soon as her niece gets here and she is able to convince her how ill she is, she will immediately bloom again She is so angry with Esther that she has to prove to her that she is very sick Whenever she does, I notice she immediately feels very strong again.

(Dear Hillary It seems to me that she is expecting and demanding that her family take the place of a village for her Do you think this is just as good?)

For Thanksgiving we arranged to go out, but her nephew invited her and they were coming to pick her up for the day She telephoned Esther in New York complaining bitterly about not wanting to go, that she wants to stay home and die and not be bothered anymore She cried - but this time Esther hung up on her. I was surprised that Dorothy was able to tell me this and I appreciated her ability to be honest about it. However it did not stop her from continuing to complain until after she went

She kept calling me to express her rage at the doctors for not being able to help her I told her that she is often angry and that is what is making her sick She insisted that she is angry only because she is sick I said "You are angry at your relatives and that makes you sick" "Wouldn't you be angry?" she answered

I realized she needed to make herself sick to get her way

with her family - something she must have done all her life She feels she is concerned about her relatives and therefore they owe her their concern.

They do keep telephoning her and she does carry-on and cry over the phone about how alone and sick she is and they express their love for her and beg her to come and live with them She said to me "There are reasons why I can't"

Dorothy wants to die in perfect health She told me about her new discovery - that when old, you do not always feel perfectly well and that doctors can't make you feel perfect forever

Dorothy was looking forward to this, Dorothy has finally decided to go and live in New York with Esther and her husband, after Ernst agreed they would live with her in Florida part of the year and take care of everything here and they would then all be together for the rest of the year in New York, where they live in a large house on a lake with boats, several automobiles and where her son with his wife and small children, as well as mother-in-law occupy apartments built onto their home Rooms were chosen by Dorothy and furnished the way she wanted. But her plans were slashed when suddenly and unexpectedly Ernst had a heart attack and died

They had brought to Florida all sorts of new kitchen appliances and everything to fully stock the kitchen for all of them They loved to cook and Dorothy was looking forward to this, and the rest of the arrangements Ernst had agreed to His death was surely a great loss to her, as well as to everyone who knew him She now felt alone and abandoned again, as she must have felt after the loss of her husband

Esther was now unable to return at once, and kept postponing doing so in order to take care of matters regarding her husband's death

Dorothy's disappointment and frustration turned into anger again She expressed this by saying to me that she was left with what she now called "their junk," and which was junking up her space - that her niece knew that she doesn't cook anymore and she therefore doesn't want these things around

She said that Ernst was supposed to take care of her and what a loss it was now to her When I said his death is a great loss to Esther too, she said, "Esther has her children and grand children." In her mind, Esther owed her for this, and she was now uncertain about wanting to stay with her any longer While she would be taken care of, she felt she would lose her independence and control

To express her hurt over what happened, she said to me that her niece left her with all this "garbage" and she wanted to throw everything out She confided in me that she now prefers to move to a residence if I would also go. This is her way in which she covers all possibilities for her survival

(Dear Hillary, Do you think she might have inherited this talent for survival from ancestors who had been raised by villages in the past?)

After some time, Esther finally told her she was coming Dorothy was very annoyed, however, that she was coming with what she called "that woman" because Esther does not like to travel by herself.

She then told me she needs to buy another pillow but doesn't want to I offered her one of mine and she accepted it only after my having to prove to her that it had been cleaned and after questioning me about my down-pillows as probably being less healthy to use then synthetic-filled ones, since she did not use down pillow anymore But after trying it out, she said to me that I have too many things and I should be glad to give things away

I later learned that she had five pillows and she could not do with one less because she felt two pillows per person was a necessity She was going to have her niece and "that woman" sleeps on her twin beds and she would sleep on the sofa bed Dorothy called it "sleeping on the floor" She was very angry that she would now have to "sleep on the floor," but she insisted on doing this

She telephoned me to come and meet her guests To my surprise I found that "that woman" called Dorothy "Auntie" most affectionately, and that they knew each other very well and for very many years since she and Esther are the grandmothers to the same small children and all live together in Esther's house in connecting apartments "That woman" is very beautiful, charming, intelligent, and most of all- or is it worst of all? - She and Esther are close and great friends This seems to be the real reason Dorothy kept hesitating about the arrangements now that Ernst was no longer there

(Dear Hillary, How does the village deal with jealousy? I would particularly like to know how this is dealt with by those who are brought up by the village compared to those who are not in the village best suited to keep jealousy from turning into rage? If not, couldn't this be a cause of wars between villages?)

This is the way Dorothy dealt with it. She insisted that Esther take all her things back and even all the food

When Esther insisted on leaving the foods which she knows Dorothy loves, she said to her. "What good is leaving me these things, I'll have to go to the supermarket to buy some anyway When I need someone to help me, there is no one - not even someone to give me a glass of water" She told me about this in a crying voice "You said that to her?" I asked "Yes I always helped everyone and there is no one to help me when I need help - not even to bring me a glass of water - I can't go to N Y to live with them I can't give up my independence" "Esther was going to be like my mother, and Ernst has to go and die Why won't they come and be here with me?"

(Dear Hillary, Dorothy must be doing something right in her way of releasing her feelings for she has been able to outlive her younger sisters Do you think she might have learned how to survive from the surrounding villages in Austria when she was a child?)

(Dear Hillary, as I read on in your book, you do say your parents had a lot of help from the village in raising your brother and you You say that your community was an extension of your family, and that you were in and out of your friends' yards and houses constantly. And that many people did their best to see that all the children in the community were getting the attention they needed

Dear Hillary, since you feel you got everything that a child needs, do you think you had the most and only exceptional village-community and which you are now proposing that every child should have? Were all the children of your village included, or were some left out? And if so, what happened to those children?

As I keep reading, I get more confused It seems to me that sometimes by "village" you mean the village you live in, and sometimes you seem to mean the whole world And sometimes the meaning of "village" seems to change to mean "the government" Is this what you mean or am I mistaken?

Sometimes I get the impression that you may have wanted to be a social worker But how did that get mixed up with political power?

You also say it takes a village to raise a child and that it takes children to raise a village In the case of Dorothy, hasn't she gotten a village of relatives to serve the same purpose?

(Dear Hillary, Is this what you want to do - to get the whole government to replace all villages to provide for all people as if they were children?)

It even seems to me that in defining "village" you ended up with including just everything But when any one thing includes everything, doesn't it nullify any particular meaning? I am now left again with not knowing what you mean

Dear Hillary,

This is what finally happened Of course Dorothy won, and although she had not wanted to go to California to be with her sister Clara, it was Clara's daughter who solved everything She told her she was coming to Florida for a very short time and would do everything necessary to move her to California with her - but this would be her last offer Phyllis said to me "Dorothy wants blood"

This niece is not only extremely intelligent and competent, but also very wealthy Besides arranging for her care, she provides her with the use of her secretary to do any chores for her - to chauffeur her to wherever she wants to go, to do any secretarial work, and whatever else she wishes. And best of all, this niece devotes one day a week to spend alone with Dorothy to entertain and nurture her, and a completely different day with her own mother to avoid any jealousy on Dorothy's part

(Dear Hillary, I wonder how much better heaven could be?)

When I spoke to her last, she finally admitted she is being treated like a Queen, the way her mother was

(Dear Hillary, could just any village have accomplished this result for Dorothy or could any government have done it better?)

(Dear Hillary, Now what about me? I met Dorothy six years ago when she was part of a "village" which did not please her, and I was alone and without any village of any kind Although we had little in common - other than being part of humanity - she was very important to me – because she was always there - and as such, she was the only one they're at my most tragic time)

(Dear Hillary, yes, I believe she was "my village"- and perhaps this one example is sufficient?)

Sincerely yours, Not Famous

Kitten On The Roof

It's no fun being a kitten, they shove me out here on the roof so I won't dirty the house It's not my fault they can't train me

I want more attention I haven't been petted and fed for hours. Perhaps if I press my face against the glass, someone will open that blue French window Meow Meow. I'll try louder. Meow Meow Meow I'm disappointed, but I'll try the other window. I'll try a quick start up that slope. I had better keep running, it is easier that way

When I run this fast, I get invigorated by the scented breeze and forget to be mad It makes me feel I am running right up over the green tree-tops into the blue ocean of sky, but the big shiny sun ball gets in my way.

I forget about food when I play with these crisp orange, green, yellow, and brown leaves They crunch when I tap them with my paw I push them, and as they slide along, I lunge to chase them, sometimes hitting them too hard and they are no longer curled

The mounds of dried pine needles are fun too when the wind blows them around I like to run after things as they move I try to catch the flies as they zigzag around me I would swallow them, but they are too fast for me

This splintering heat makes me want some cold milk, and the sticky tar burns my paws. Even the graceful and languid stretching of my gray and white body gives me no satisfaction

I hear pots being moved, and I smell fried onions and meat I am getting excited I can't keep still. I stand up on my hind legs and continue trying to climb up the window even though I keep falling down I tare at the panels with my clenched paws and extended nails I wiggle and squirm so hard I scream wildly, not caring how ugly it makes me look Finally I scratch on the glass window fiercely, for that usually gets results

They're pretending they don't hear me even though I felt I was pushing right through the window I'm worn out. I'll sit still and squint, my eyes and narrow my face in anger, collapse by body, straighten my whiskers, and sensuously wave my tail very, very low

I hear someone opening the window!

Poems

I Think Of Silence

I think of silence when my nerves are infected with the
hyperactivity of jiggling music
I think of silence when I am imprisoned in the violent
noises of out underground dungeons, the subways
Most of all I think of the vow of silence as the only possible
therapy for friendly acquaintances, who gift me with their
endless circular (circuitous) talk that never stops

Times Square

The lights twinkle their stars into your soul and twinkle
them out through your eyes
They wrap you in jewels, and follow you breathing with
your movements
And rhyming with your heart

As Students In New York

Teachers, teachers everywhere
And not a thought to think Teachers, teachers everywhere
Over methods we make a stink
What if we had an idea, a thought - do you suppose -
Would happen to our methods bought
At twenty dollars a point, in diplomas sealed? New ways
would automatically grow
And leave behind this dirth congealed?
Oh water, water everywhere
We need to wash this teaching profession and make of all
its preaching air
A non- prostituted confession
Why do teachers cheat and lie
When teachers become students in this college? For fortune
they must show their grades of courage Bandaged round
these marks to show
How many friends their papers owe
Frightened pupils they become when they their teaching
Masks do drop - filled with authoritarian steel
Their veins in stiffness must they hold
To prove their ability to mark and fold Compulsives act to
keep themselves from seeing
What uselessness to society they make of beings
Farewell, farewell, but this I tell
We need to wash this teaching profession He prayeth well
who loveth well
A non-prostituted confession

Money Honey

I can't give you anything but money
Love is unfit for humankind
There's no new world paved with love to fin
For all, this world is seemingly so sunny
Every maiden yet cries out for love
Goes through life picking of its flowers
Always seeking something that's above instead of picturing
greenbacks in her bowers
The world's as old as money, it is true, let's not forsake it
Romance, youth and love wither and die
Let's abide it, it is so much more clever
To fall in love with money, that goes on forever and ever
Youth and love wither and die, romantic
Love's paved with poets' anguish, gripping, frantic
There's no new world paved with honey
No, our new world has not been paved with love
Our brave new world still finds that love is blind
So I can't give you anything but money, Honey
Love is not something fit for us to find
Still, the entire world cries out for love, for love
Yet it is money they're thinking of
Instead of love, foolish, foolish little flowers
Can't they picture greenbacks in their bowers?
Our world has grown old with money Youth and love
wither and die, funny

But age goes on forever ever
Let us abide, it is much more clever
To just fall in love with money, forever Money, Honey,
Funny, ever and ever

It's The System

Do you know who's to blame? Not you, not me. It's the System!

The terrible, terrible system

If I do bad, it's the fault of the System, But if I do good, it's never the System

If I don't have enough to eat, it's the fault of the System

If I eat too much, is it the System?

If you're going to tell me it's my responsibility, I can just smile and say, "No, it's the System"

The terrible, terrible system!

Don't tell on me, and I won't tell on you

Remember, we have the system. So let's call everything the System

The terrible, terrible system!

Who me? No never me.

Not you or me It's the System!

I Hold My Breath Alone

I hold my breath when I am told I should be like everyone
I hold my breath when I am asked for my opinion that is
not even heard or listened to
I hold my breath when people quote me so inaccurately that
it is hopeless to try and correct it
I hold my breath when people attribute to me what they
themselves want to believe
I hold my breath when I hear demands and criticisms of
others, which are unfair
I hold my breath when I feel harangued by empty repetitious
opinions
I hold my breath when I say, "You are right" to help someone
stop from continuing to say what is not right.
I hold my breath, and suffer the consequences, even more -
from holding my breath
I start to breath when I distance myself enough to observe
and realize that all people are what they are, just as I am
what I am, and try to understand.
Alone
We Are Alone, As Jesus Was Deserted By All, As Jesus
Was
Morality and Justice Are Equated with Oil
Now it's Oil, Oil, Oil
We are Again
Alone, Alone, Alone As Jesus Was

The Heavens

Life stretched itself over a mountain, touched hands with the stars, and threw them over the heavens It picked up the planets and with strings around their centers, tied them all around the moon, causing the moon to fly wildly and ecstatically over the skies

Then to calm them, life slapped its hands against the waters of the sun. Below a fierce streak of fire struck through the skies It struck through the elements that had previously risen proudly through the skies

The trees blew ice all over the smoke, but the fire climbed the skies while walking the earth into the tunnels The windows of the world crashed, and the panes flew by the birds onto a fountain of blood

The fire curled around the forests and dug life into the ground. The heavens in turn curled themselves over the black smoke and fought hard for the keys of the kingdom

Truth danced and cried for the life that had fallen through The torn pages of life were now walking the floors of the sky Madness was tipping its red false hats to the sun

The sun and the stars then held hands and cried for the truth that had fallen down into the mud The lights went out but something flew over the trees and played music over the whisperings of the moon

END

Printed in the United States
By Bookmasters